BIBLE PRAYERS
For Women

Publications International, Ltd.

Photography from Getty Images and Shutterstock.com

ISBN: 978-1-64030-115-3

Manufactured in China.

8 7 6 5 4 3 2 1

TABLE OF *Contents*

GUIDANCE

*And the Lord said, I have pardoned
according to thy word: But as truly as I live,
all the earth shall be filled with the
glory of the Lord.*

—Numbers 14:20–21

Lord, the best way
I know to say thank you for
your wonderful guidance
is to try to be the kind of
person you have taught me
to be. Please continue to lift
me up every day as I strive
to be my best self.

*Blessed are the pure in heart:
for they shall see God.*

—Matthew 5:8

How can I be pure in heart, Lord? I certainly don't always have right thoughts and motives. Perhaps being pure in heart can happen through being honest about what's going on inside my heart and working to purify it. I can make it a point to focus on what is right and true and good, continually turning my heart toward you to find those things and be renewed in them. That's why I'm here right now, Lord. Purify my heart as I walk close to you today and enjoy the blessing of fellowship with you.

In all thy ways acknowledge him, and he shall direct thy paths.

—*Proverbs 3:6*

Each day, I face dozens of decisions, big and small. The small ones are usually easy, like what to defrost for dinner, or which PJs I want to wear to bed. The bigger ones are not quite as easy, especially when they involve outcomes that directly affect my family or friends. I must remind myself throughout the day to stop and think—what would God want me to do? God's will is always the right decision, even if it isn't the one I might have chosen. I can honestly say on several occasions, my own stubbornness and limited perception made problems worse, not better. God, I ask that you always direct my choices and guide my thoughts. I ask that your ways become my ways in everything I do.

Then shall the King say unto them on his right hand, Come, ye blessed of my Father, inherit the kingdom prepared for you from the foundation of the world.

—Matthew 25:34

I wonder who I will be today. Will I be the woman, the individual spirit with individual hopes and dreams? Will I be the loving and supportive wife? Maybe I'll be called upon to be the good friend, the one who listens and offers sage advice. Will I be the perfect employee, who gets the job done right and on time? I imagine I will also have to be the mother, who cleans up after and prods along and scolds and loves and forgives. Then again, it will probably be a day just like any other, when I will be called upon to be all these things and more. Lord, no matter what this day brings, help me get through it with your loving guidance.

*I am the good shepherd,
and know my sheep,
and am known of mine.*

—John 10:14

Your Word says—and I've heard it elsewhere—that a flock of sheep knows its own shepherd's voice and won't respond to the voice of a different shepherd. It's true of my relationship with you, too, Lord. I know your voice. I know when you're speaking to my heart, and I know when I'm being coaxed by "other voices"—wrong desires, worldly values, anxiety, pride, and the like. Thanks for helping me see the difference. Coax me to follow the sound of your voice today and always.

*Therefore I esteem all thy precepts
concerning all things to be right;
and I hate every false way.*

—*Psalm 119:128*

Lord, teach me to think ahead about the results my actions might inflict. If things go awry despite my forethought, help me admit my wrongs and right them. Amen.

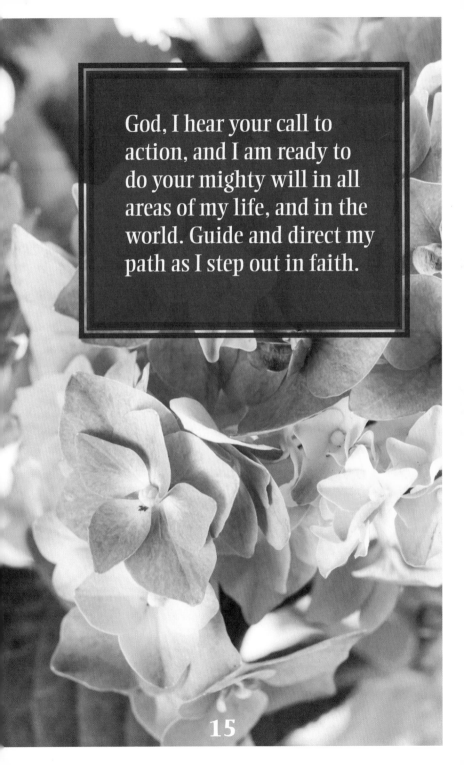

God, I hear your call to action, and I am ready to do your mighty will in all areas of my life, and in the world. Guide and direct my path as I step out in faith.

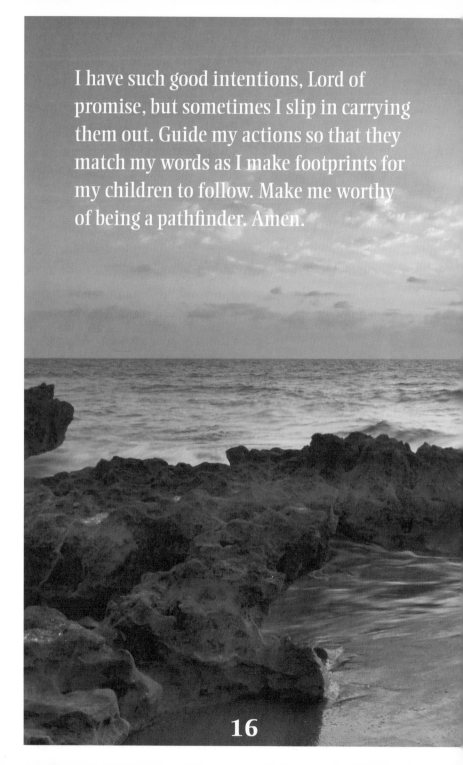

I have such good intentions, Lord of promise, but sometimes I slip in carrying them out. Guide my actions so that they match my words as I make footprints for my children to follow. Make me worthy of being a pathfinder. Amen.

But why dost thou judge thy brother?
or why dost thou set at nought thy brother?
for we shall all stand before the
judgment seat of Christ.

—Romans 14:10

When I am on social media, I start to feel depressed after awhile. So much negativity, and so much judgment between people! Yet we are told not to judge others, because we will then be judged in return. God is the only judge there is, yet I see so many people playing judge, jury, and executioner for the sins and mistakes of others. God, help us all to remember that judging is itself a sin, because it comes from pride and ego, and not from love and compassion. Help us, God, to open our hearts to those who stumble, not humiliate them. Help us remember we are all going to one day stand in judgment to you, God, the only one that matters.

And now the Lord shew kindness and truth unto you: and I also will requite you this kindness, because ye have done this thing.

—*2 Samuel 2:6*

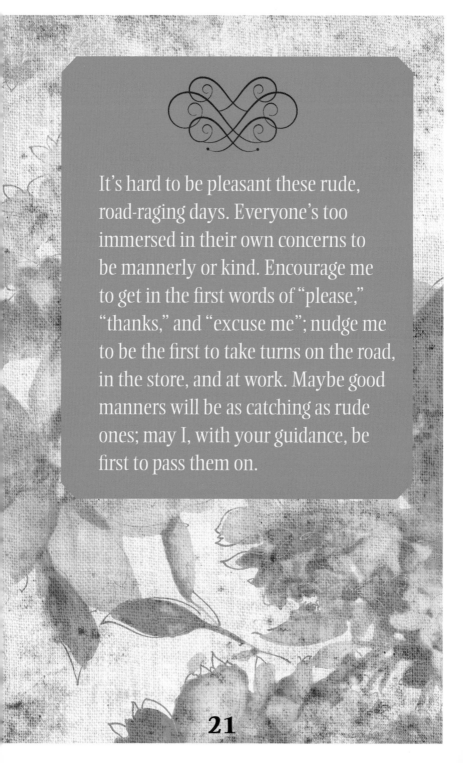

It's hard to be pleasant these rude, road-raging days. Everyone's too immersed in their own concerns to be mannerly or kind. Encourage me to get in the first words of "please," "thanks," and "excuse me"; nudge me to be the first to take turns on the road, in the store, and at work. Maybe good manners will be as catching as rude ones; may I, with your guidance, be first to pass them on.

To every thing there is a season, and a time to every purpose under the heaven.

—Ecclesiastes 3:1

Dear God, I thank you for the opportunity to do both of the things I love: being a mother and holding down a meaningful job. It has been hectic, Lord, and sometimes I wonder if my job is worth the late nights and weekends spent doing laundry and housework. I become so tired I can barely function. I need your steadying hand, Father. I need you to help me discern what I can and cannot do. I need you to make the pieces fit. You help me find balance in my day—to find a time for every purpose. After school and evenings are for my kids and husband; late nights and Saturdays are for chores. I wait for Sundays, Lord, to be with you and renew myself in worship. I could not accomplish anything without your sweet spirit blowing through me, refreshing and strengthening me each day so I can give my best to my family and my job.

Judge not, that ye be not judged.

—Matthew 7:1

Dear Lord, I have a daughter in middle school. She and her friends are coming into their own, trying to figure out who they are. Technology makes it even simpler to be unkind, and it is tempting to adopt a judgmental attitude in order to fit in with others. God, help me guide my children as they navigate this time of change and growth. Please protect my family from the ways of the judgmental, and from adopting those ways in their interactions with others.

For the promise is unto you, and to your children, and to all that are afar off, even as many as the Lord our God shall call.

—Acts 2:39

Lord, how we cling to your promise that the Holy Spirit is always near to all who believe in you. How comforting it is for us as parents to know that our children have the Holy Spirit to guide them and lead them into a purposeful life. We praise you, Lord, for your loving care for us and for our children and grandchildren.

He that covereth a transgression seeketh love; but he that repeateth a matter separateth very friends.

—Proverbs 17:9

No matter how hard I try, God of guidance, some-one finds fault with me. I am mortified about the latest criticism. I can't decide whether to run away in shame or storm back and defend my actions, for I thought I was right. Criticism hurts most when coupled with ridicule, and I feel like less of a person for the tone in which I was ad-dressed. Give me the courage to confront this, Lord, for it is not acceptable to be treated this way even when in error. Keep me calm, factual, and open; perhaps the tone was unintentional, the critic unaware of the power of shaming. Help me remember how I feel now the next time I find fault with someone. As I've learned first-hand with you the zillions of times I messed up, there are better ways to confront mistakes than with stinging criticisms that divide and demean. Truth be known, Lord, such abrasive manners say more about the criticizer than the criticized. Keep me from passing them on.

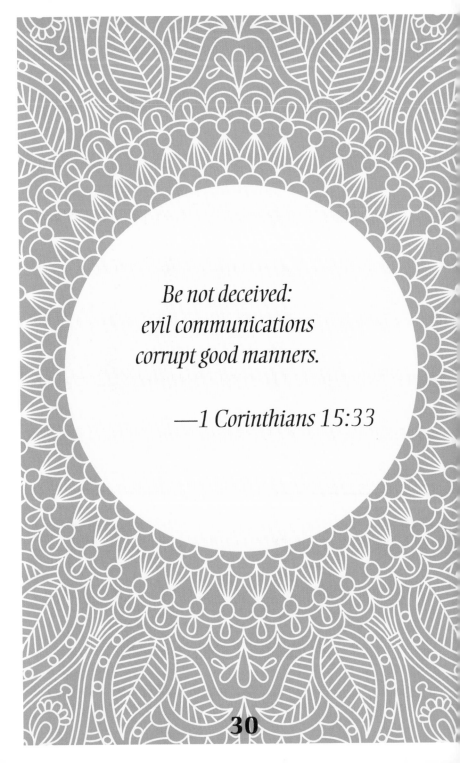

Be not deceived:
evil communications
corrupt good manners.

—1 Corinthians 15:33

I appreciate the connections made possible by social media, but I also recognize that like everything else, when it comes to technology, moderation is key. Yesterday I was glued to a series of screens throughout the day, from phone to laptop, and when I tore myself away to make dinner, I found myself in a particularly ill mood. While I had happily corresponded with an old friend who lives on another continent, I'd also witnessed a good deal of negativity, judgmental attitudes, and blatantly hateful behavior online. The prolonged exposure had soured my spirit, and when I snapped at my son, I realized that my choices that day did not benefit my family or me. God, help me to capitalize on the good inherent in technology, while also practicing moderation and sound judgment. Do not let me fall prey to the negativity that can be part of the online experience.

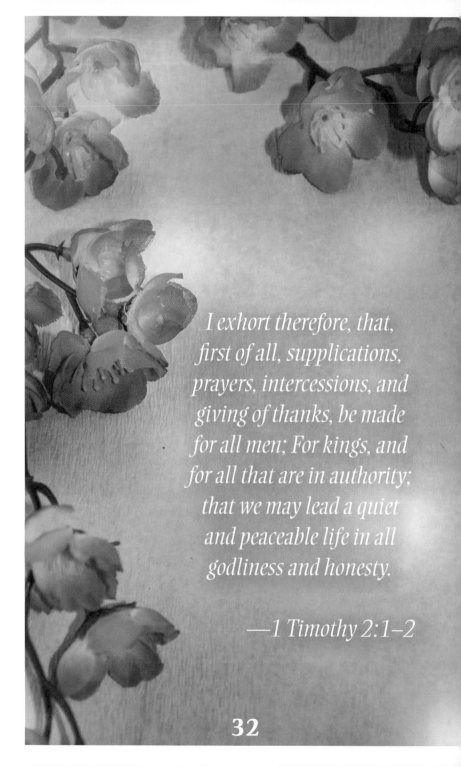

I exhort therefore, that,
first of all, supplications,
prayers, intercessions, and
giving of thanks, be made
for all men; For kings, and
for all that are in authority;
that we may lead a quiet
and peaceable life in all
godliness and honesty.

—1 Timothy 2:1–2

Life is full of trade-offs, Lord, and I need to make one. Guide my search for a career where I can have both a life and a living. Your balance is not found running in a circle, but along a beckoning path where enough is more than sufficient; where money comes second to family, community, and self; where success takes on new meaning; and where, in the giving up, I gain wealth beyond belief.

If we live in the Spirit, let us also walk in the Spirit.

—Galatians 5:25

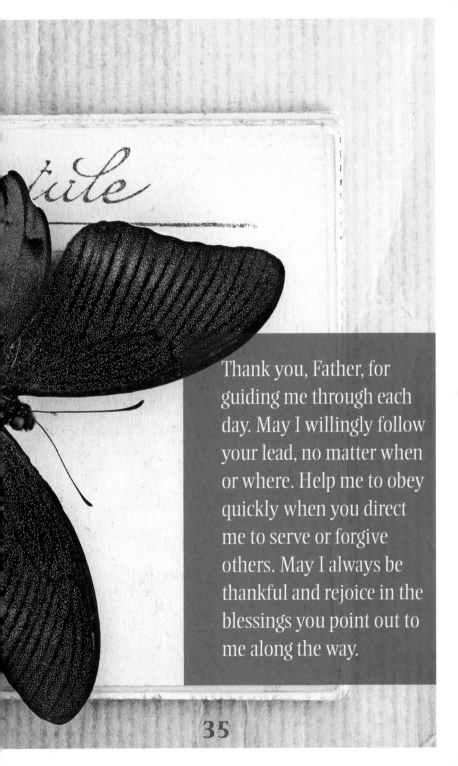

Thank you, Father, for guiding me through each day. May I willingly follow your lead, no matter when or where. Help me to obey quickly when you direct me to serve or forgive others. May I always be thankful and rejoice in the blessings you point out to me along the way.

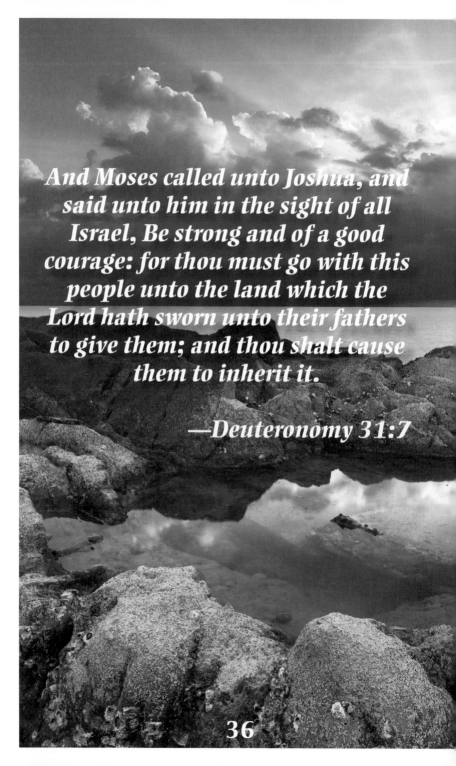

And Moses called unto Joshua, and said unto him in the sight of all Israel, Be strong and of a good courage: for thou must go with this people unto the land which the Lord hath sworn unto their fathers to give them; and thou shalt cause them to inherit it.

—Deuteronomy 31:7

Danielle's mother, Olivia, had always been the matriarch, the "glue" that held her family together. When Olivia was diagnosed with Parkinson's disease, Danielle, as the eldest of her siblings, knew she needed to step up and be strong for everyone. "I suddenly was called upon to mediate and make decisions that affected the entire family," Danielle remembers. "It was ultimately a time of growth, but I felt challenged. I prayed for guidance a lot." Dear God, please embolden me to be a leader, just as Moses uplifted Joshua to lead the Israelites into the promised land.

Keep thy heart with all diligence; for out of it are the issues of life.

—Proverbs 4:23

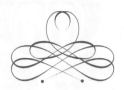

God, we live in a fast-moving time. There are so many distractions; the very tools that help us navigate our days can also unhinge us. How many times have I interrupted my husband as he shared a story in service to an incoming call or text? How many times have I multitasked admirably, taking advantage of all that the digital world allows, but in the process neglected mindfulness—ignoring the flesh-and-blood people with whom I shared a room? It is impossible to be present and listen fully when I have one eye on my phone. God, please help me to retain my priorities, to give the people I am with my full love and attention—my undivided self. May I always protect my heart and listen with my heart.

For sin shall not have dominion over you: for ye are not under the law, but under grace.

—Romans 6:14

Oh, how we women love to beat ourselves up for not being perfect! I am harder on myself than anyone else and my high expectations sometimes leave me exhausted and defeated. I nitpick at myself for every little thing I do wrong. But God doesn't judge me by my imperfections. In his eyes, I am perfect as long as I do my best, even if I stumble a bit on the way. God, never let me forget your grace is my perfection, and your love my only expectation. Help me to see myself as you see me, made in your image, and a reflection of your love in the physical world. I may make mistakes and miss the mark sometimes, but my aim, and my heart, is true, God.

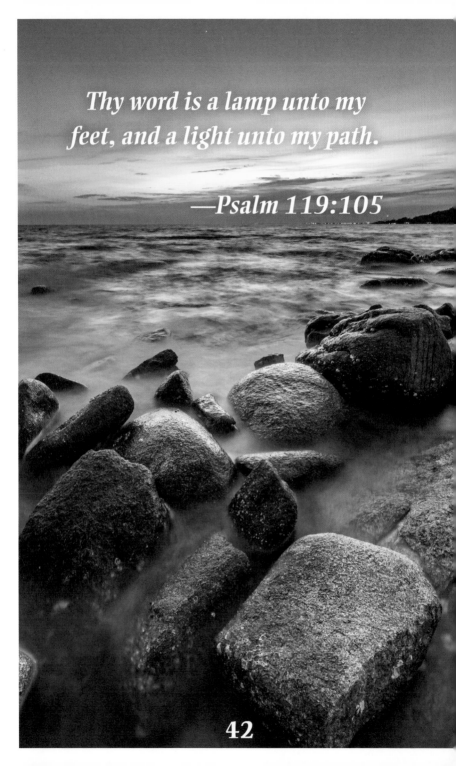

Thy word is a lamp unto my feet, and a light unto my path.

—Psalm 119:105

42

As a college student living in the United States, I have many advantages, and it's easy to fall into the trap of feeling that, given all I have going for me, I should "be the best at everything." I am hard on myself when I don't get the best grade, for example, or when I perceive that I'm not as physically attractive as some of the girls in the dorm. God, help me to remember that there is always room for improvement, a condition I share with everyone else on Earth, and that your Word can comfort me, guide me, and serve as the ultimate "self improvement manual."

We ask for guidance in all the decisions we must make in the days ahead, the big decisions, and even the little daily ones. We acknowledge that without divine direction, our lives become meaningless, wrapped in our own selfishness, heading nowhere. Lead us where you want us go!

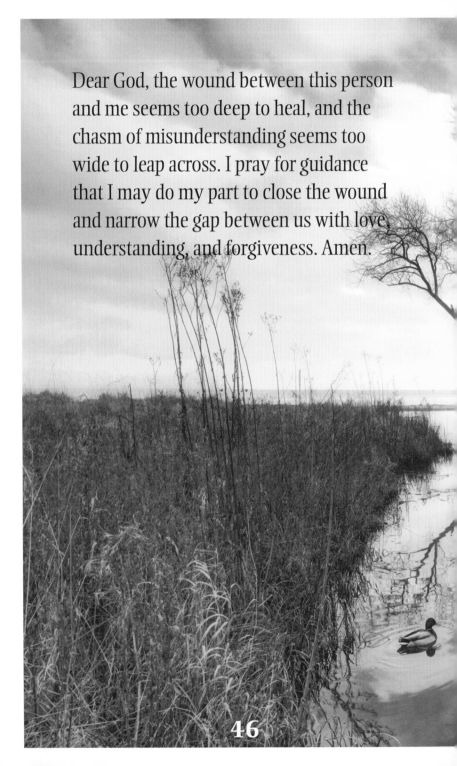

Dear God, the wound between this person and me seems too deep to heal, and the chasm of misunderstanding seems too wide to leap across. I pray for guidance that I may do my part to close the wound and narrow the gap between us with love, understanding, and forgiveness. Amen.

When I feel my control slipping, Lord, I
know I only have to call on you for encouragement, direction, and guidance to get your
loving assistance.

HOPE

For we through the Spirit wait for the
hope of righteousness by faith.

—*Galatians 5:5*

Dear Lord, I am feeling more hopeful these days. For awhile, I forgot to include your loving guidance and grace in my life. I forgot that if I pray and meditate and just get silent enough to listen, you always give me the answers I seek, and the direction I need to overcome anything life hands me. I pray for continued guidance and wisdom, and that I may always live from a place of hope instead of fear, and a place of possibilities instead of limitations. You are my wings and my rock, allowing me to both soar higher and stay grounded. No matter what I may be facing, staying in the comforting light of your presence gives me the hope I need to carry on with my head held high and my heart strong and fearless. Thank you for the gift of hope. Amen.

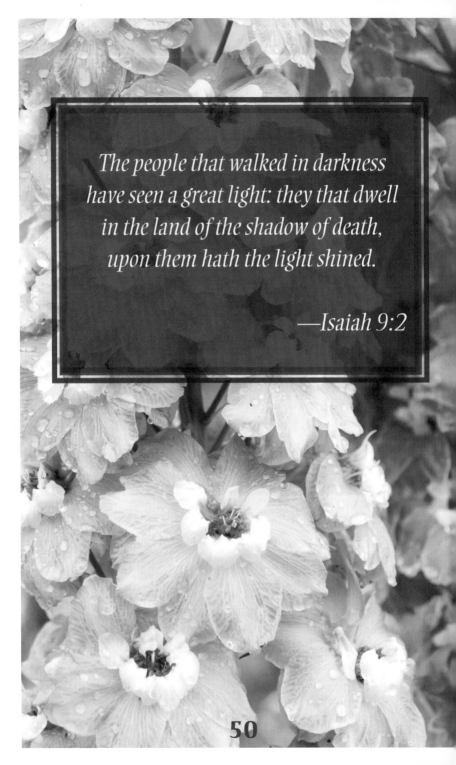

The people that walked in darkness have seen a great light: they that dwell in the land of the shadow of death, upon them hath the light shined.

—Isaiah 9:2

The prophet Isaiah wrote a number of inspired words from God that pointed to the coming of Christ to Earth. In this passage, he speaks of a great light shining on those living in a dark land. Spiritual darkness is the deepest kind of darkness. One may live in the darkness of being physically blind and yet have the light of Christ, which brings meaning, joy, and hope. Without the light of Christ in a life, there is something missing in the soul.

*Be of good courage, and he shall strengthen
your heart, all ye that hope in the Lord.*

—Psalm 31:24

Losing a loved one is never easy. I've always been the strong person in the family, able to handle things while everyone around me fell apart. But sometimes I lose my way and feel like I could break down. That is when I have to look deep within my heart to find courage and resilience, because death brings out all my deepest fears. That is when I must turn to God to be my hope and my comforter, and to hold me up when I feel like falling. My hope is rewarded with God's love, and allows me to become strong again and help my family cope with the loss in the most loving and caring manner possible. My hope is God.

I wait for the Lord, my soul doth wait,
and in his word do I hope.

—Psalm 130:5

Lord, help me remember that you are the God of hope. You don't want me to feel sad or hopeless. It isn't your plan for me to live in fear or doubt. Help me to feel and access the power of the Holy Spirit. I know that through your Spirit I will find the hope and joy and peace you have promised to your people.

In our worst moments, shattered by pain in body, mind, and spirit, God has promised not to leave us alone or without comfort.

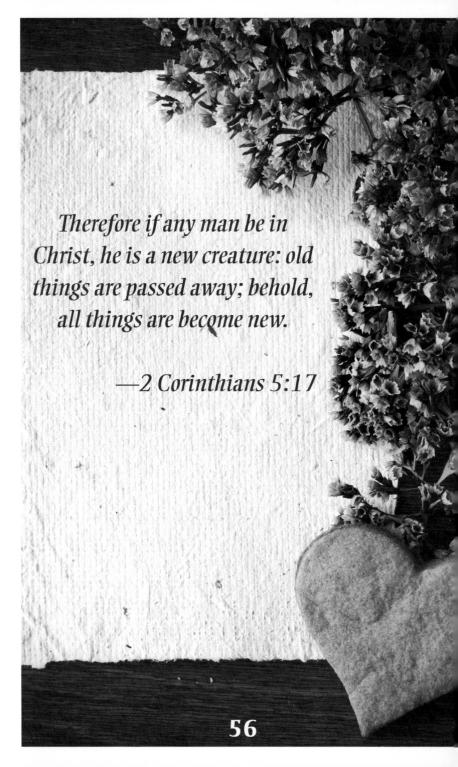

Therefore if any man be in Christ, he is a new creature: old things are passed away; behold, all things are become new.

—2 Corinthians 5:17

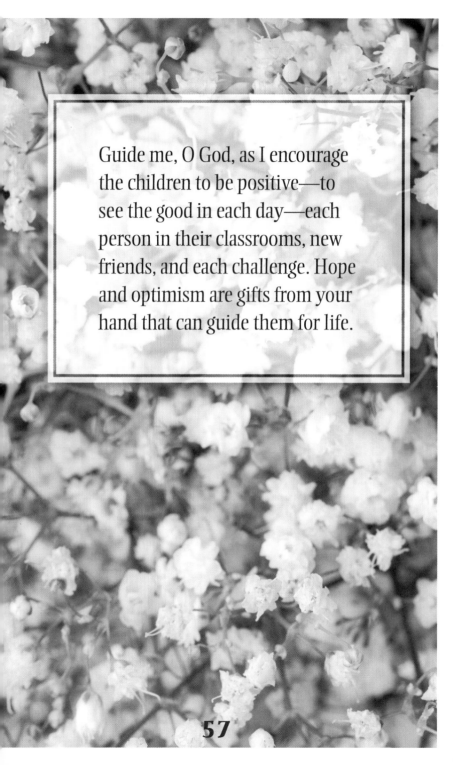

Guide me, O God, as I encourage
the children to be positive—to
see the good in each day—each
person in their classrooms, new
friends, and each challenge. Hope
and optimism are gifts from your
hand that can guide them for life.

Lord, although we are often not certain of your intentions when you present us with unpleasant circumstances, we understand that you do have a reason. The hurt isn't just to spite us. Please help us to keep our outlooks positive and allow us to aid others who are as dismayed and in just as much pain as we are. Amen.

Being confident of this very thing, that he which hath begun a good work in you will perform it until the day of Jesus Christ.

—Philippians 1:6

"Another close call," Bridget said glumly. Bridget is an actress, and she was referring to a recent audition in which she almost, but didn't, get a plum role. "But God has my back," she added, brightening. "I just need to be patient, and stay the course. I've got the skills. I work hard. My time will come!" Dear Lord, it can be frustrating when I reach high and don't seem to succeed. Help me to be patient and remember that you work with us all our lives, just on your time!

And Sarah said, God hath made me to laugh, so that all that hear will laugh with me.

—Genesis 21:6

As we face worrisome days, restore our funny bones, Lord. Humor helps rebuild and heal, sparking hope and igniting energy with which to combat stress, ease grief, and provide direction.

Almighty God, I know you are supremely faithful! Today I ask you to restore hope to the hopeless. Plant seeds of hope in hearts that have lain fallow for so long. Send down showers of hope on those struggling with illness, persecution, or difficult relationships. Hope that comes from you is hope with the power to sustain us when nothing around us seems the least bit hopeful.

Blessed is the man that trusteth in the Lord, and whose hope the Lord is.

—Jeremiah 17:7

Living in difficult times requires us to maintain a positive, hopeful attitude about the future. Having hope is vital for our mental, physical, and spiritual health. Lord, help me move into the future with a steadfast spirit, looking forward in faith and hope and trusting in the promises you have made to your people. Today I make a covenant to you that I will choose hope. If I encounter disappointment, I will choose hope. If confronted with temptation, I will choose hope. In the face of fear, I will choose hope. If I sense doubt washing over me, I will choose hope. If I feel angry, I will choose hope. Instead of giving in to sadness or despair, I will choose hope. In all things that come my way today, Lord, I am determined to choose hope. Regardless of what happened in the past, today—through you—I am strong enough to choose hope.

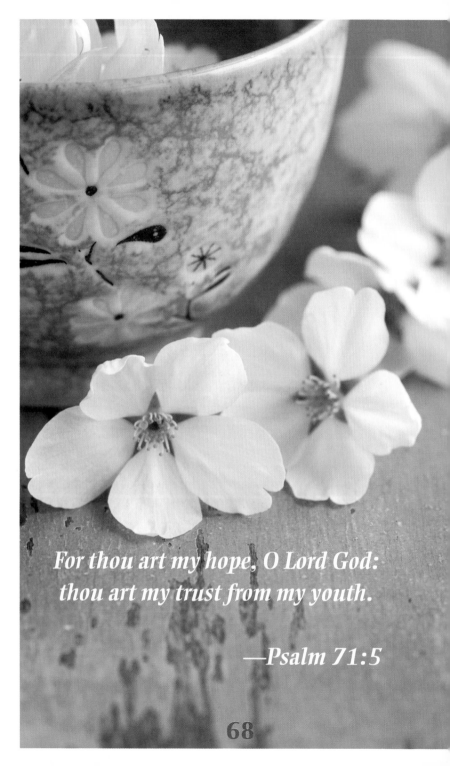

For thou art my hope, O Lord God:
thou art my trust from my youth.

—Psalm 71:5

Little children automatically see the good and look for the silver linings. Kids have such hope built into their personalities. I recall when I was young, I had faith and hope that all would be well, even when my parents or family suffered some illness, job loss, or other hardship. I just had that seed of hope in my heart. Now that I am older, I find my hope in God and his presence and love. I still feel that sense of goodness and that all will be well when I am centered in hope and in him. If I keep my heart open, as I did when I was little, and come to God for help, he never fails to give me what I need.

Let us hold fast the profession of our faith without wavering; (for he is faithful that promised).

—*Hebrews 10:23*

Like a speed bump in a parking lot, a decision lies in our path, placed there by God to remind us hope is a choice. Choosing to live as people of hope is not to diminish or belittle pain and suffering or lie about evil's reality. Rather it is to cling to God's promise that he will make all things new.

Wherefore gird up the loins of your mind, be sober, and hope to the end for the grace that is to be brought unto you at the revelation of Jesus Christ.

—1 Peter 1:13

Father, your Word makes it clear to me that the life of faith is not passive. While we wait for you to answer prayer, grant wisdom, and open doors, we also keep our minds sharp and our hearts strengthened by reading and studying your Word, by meeting with you in prayer, and by finding encouragement among other believers. These are the disciplines our souls need to stay focused on ever-present hope.

Things happen in life that level us. When we suffer a disaster or a loved one dies, it feels as though we will never smile again. We die a little, too. God, my faith and belief in your eternal love and compassion is what gets me through these little deaths, and saves me so that I can indeed live to smile another day. I am grateful for every moment of life you've blessed me with, including the days I suffer, because without them, I am not able to feel the full extent of the rebirth I experience when the light returns. With every ending, a new beginning is possible with you, dear God, at my side.

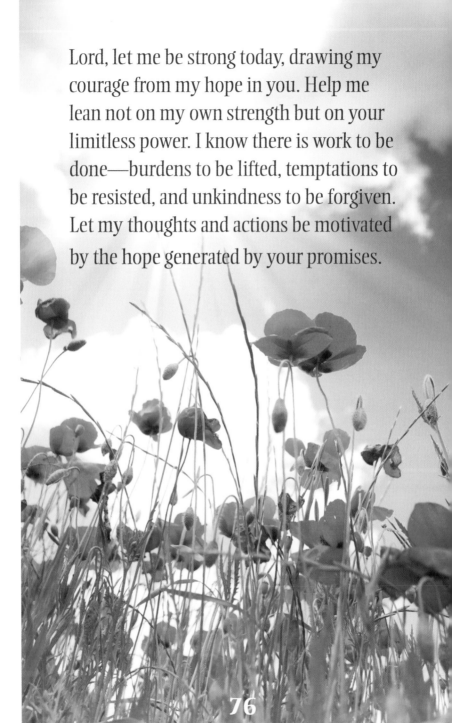

Lord, let me be strong today, drawing my courage from my hope in you. Help me lean not on my own strength but on your limitless power. I know there is work to be done—burdens to be lifted, temptations to be resisted, and unkindness to be forgiven. Let my thoughts and actions be motivated by the hope generated by your promises.

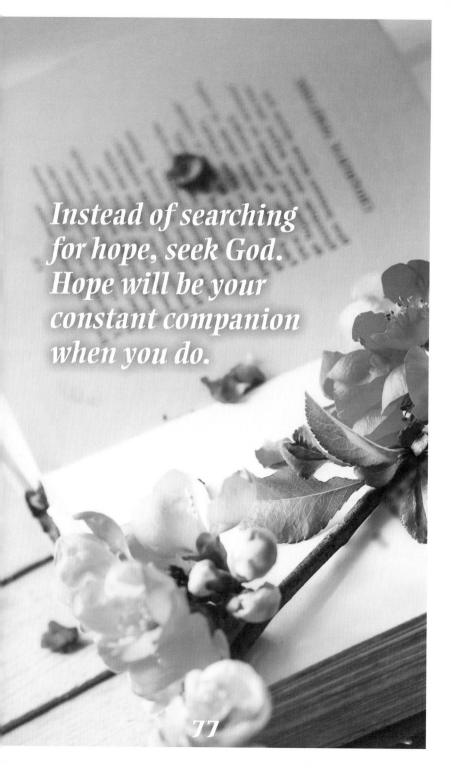

Instead of searching for hope, seek God. Hope will be your constant companion when you do.

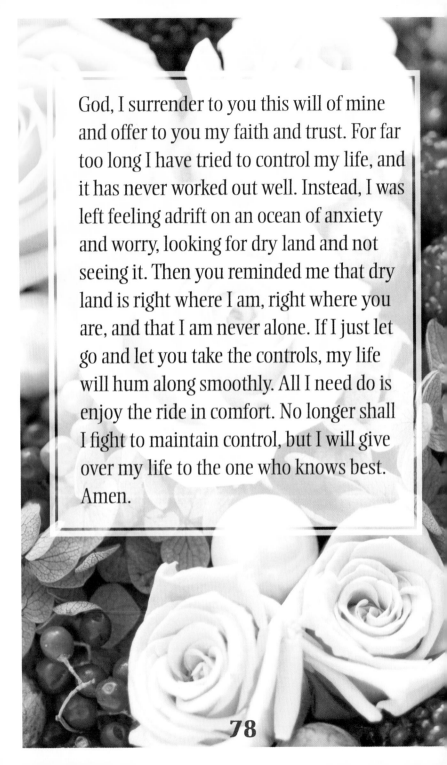

God, I surrender to you this will of mine and offer to you my faith and trust. For far too long I have tried to control my life, and it has never worked out well. Instead, I was left feeling adrift on an ocean of anxiety and worry, looking for dry land and not seeing it. Then you reminded me that dry land is right where I am, right where you are, and that I am never alone. If I just let go and let you take the controls, my life will hum along smoothly. All I need do is enjoy the ride in comfort. No longer shall I fight to maintain control, but I will give over my life to the one who knows best. Amen.

Hope knows that in the midst of feeling all alone, God is still with me.

Jesus said unto her, I am the resurrection, and the life: he that believeth in me, though he were dead, yet shall he live: And whosoever liveth and believeth in me shall never die.

—John 11:25–26

Lord, I do believe! And because of my hope of life with you in eternity, there is all the more meaning for life today. There's meaning in my choices, my relationships, my work, my play, and my worship. It all matters, it all counts, and I live knowing one day I'll stand in your presence with great joy.

Creator God, you have come to me with healing in your hand. When I cried out, you heard me. You provided me with a gift that brought both peace and pleasure to my harried life. You helped me to focus on life instead of illness and sorrow. Lord, thank you for this wondrous gift. Amen.

The hope of the righteous shall be gladness: but the expectation of the wicked shall perish.

—Proverbs 10:28

I see people every day doing wrong and bringing harm to others, and benefiting from it. I see good people suffering and losing everything, and I wonder where the justice is. Lord, help me remember your justice happens on a much higher level and that the hope of the good is always rewarded, while the motives of the evil are always judged and accounted for. Let me not have any expectations that come from a place of selfishness or greed, but help me, Lord, to always hope to be my best, and do my best, for myself and others. If I walk the right path, I may still suffer, but I know my ultimate reward will be joy. May I always walk the right path, Lord.

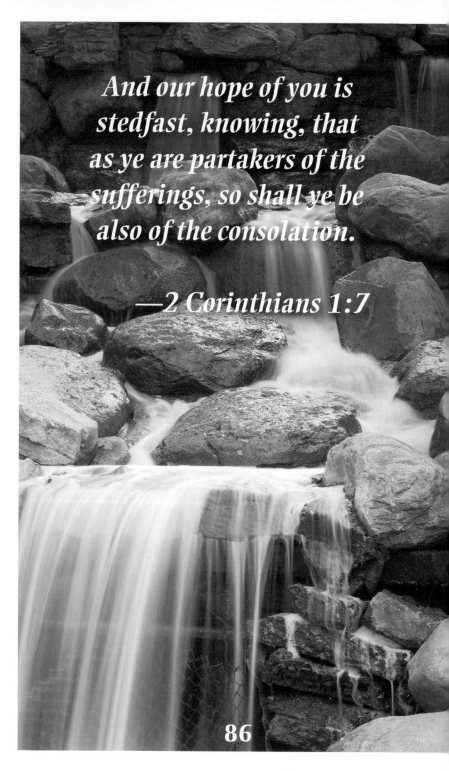

And our hope of you is stedfast, knowing, that as ye are partakers of the sufferings, so shall ye be also of the consolation.

—2 Corinthians 1:7

Why me, Lord? I have asked that question so many times, when I become ill, or one of my children is hurt. Why me, Lord? And his answer? Why not you? I learned the Lord doesn't pick and choose who suffers. We all suffer at some point in life, and no one is immune. But I also learned whatever suffering the Lord asks me to experience comes with the courage, strength, and compassion to get through it. It's a promise the Lord made to me, that he would never give me more than I could handle. So when things come into my life I'd rather not deal with, I have hope and faith that I can deal with them, with the Lord to guide me.

For the Lord thy God bringeth thee into a good land, a land of brooks of water, of fountains and depths that spring out of valleys and hills.

—Deuteronomy 8:7–9

God, when I am tired and just feeling down about everything in my life, your love reminds me that there is a spring of hope and renewal I can drink from anytime. It may take me awhile to come around, but I always come back to love as the reason to keep on going, even when my gas tank is empty. Love fuels me and gets me back out on the road of life, ready for whatever new challenge you have in store for me.

Lord, I'm looking forward to this new phase of my life. It is full of promise and hope, though I know that challenges will surely come as well. I know you have all the courage, strength, faithfulness, and love I need to meet each moment from a perspective of peace. I just need to stay tethered to you in prayer, listening for your Spirit to guide me and turn my thoughts continually back toward you. That's the key to a good life.

There are few things in life more heart-breaking than the death of a child. One so recently born, exiting life far too soon for our hearts to handle it. A time to be born, and a time to die. But there's supposed to be lots of time in between—a lifetime, in fact. How do we pick up the pieces and go on when our hearts ache as they never have before? O Lord, it is so hard to see the hope in certain circumstances. I guess we just need time. Time to grieve. Time to regain our balance. Time to renew our trust and hope for the future. While we are going through this season of healing, please hold us close.

Now our Lord Jesus Christ himself, and God, even our Father, which hath loved us, and hath given us everlasting consolation and good hope through grace, Comfort your hearts, and stablish you in every good word and work.

—*2 Thessalonians 2:16–17*

Dear God, your heavenly grace has rescued me from the darkness and brought me into the light again. Each time I'm reminded of your miraculous presence in my life, the light gets brighter and problems melt away. I know then that you have touched me with a special, loving touch that makes my heart sing out with joy just to be alive. Knowing that you deem me worthy of your grace renews my strength and hope that all will be well in my life. Thank you, God.

FAMILY

Hereby perceive we the love of God, because he laid down his life for us: and we ought to lay down our lives for the brethren. But whoso hath this world's good, and seeth his brother have need, and shutteth up his bowels of compassion from him, how dwelleth the love of God in him?

—1 John 3:16–17

The love and devotion of family serves as the foundation upon which faith is built and cherished. The support of family acts both as wings to fly and a safety net to catch us. The honesty and trustworthiness of family creates both sanctuary and accountability for each of us in our journeys.

*Children, obey your parents
in all things: for this is well
pleasing unto the Lord.*

—Colossians 3:20

Dear Lord, I am officially in the "Sandwich Generation," raising my own children while helping my parents navigate the challenges of aging. Dad has developed Parkinson's, and Mom's arthritis is getting worse. My husband and I are devoted to helping them with practical matters like getting to the doctor, cleaning their home, and buying groceries, and I have recently started bringing my older daughter along when we run errands with Mom. The challenges my folks face make me keenly aware of life's cycles of loss and change. I know my daughter feels it, too. But my hope is that these dates with Mom might be a way to demonstrate to my daughter what respect for elders can mean. Aging is a part of being, and compassion is an important lesson. Dear God, help me set the right example for my children through my relationship with my own parents.

Beloved, if God so loved us, we ought also to love one another.

—1 John 4:11

Lord, we want to honor the grandparents who tended us so well. Pause with us as we play again in the dusty lanes of childhood at Grandma and Grandpa's house. Bless these bigger-than-life companions who helped us bridge home and away, childhood and maturity. In their footsteps, we made the journey. Thank you for such a heritage and an opportunity to express our gratitude.

And if one prevail against him, two shall withstand him; and a threefold cord is not quickly broken.

—Ecclesiastes 4:12

My husband and I don't attend church every Sunday, but each weekend we make time to read scripture and talk about the week, which we try to view through the lens of spirituality. A difficult coworker, good news in our extended families—we'll discuss the good and the bad and talk about how God informs each ebb and flow. Sometimes we'll share a joy, such as the time my husband built a new bird feeder and we both discovered the great calm and pleasure we derived from watching the sparrows and finches. I think we both gain a lot from these quiet, regular moments of sharing. The Bible reminds me how your presence in my life, and my husband's life, creates a powerful "threefold cord." God, if my marriage is grounded in you, it will be strong.

Bless this partnership, God, the friendship of me and my partner for life. And remind us both: Every gathering of two is really a fellowship of three.

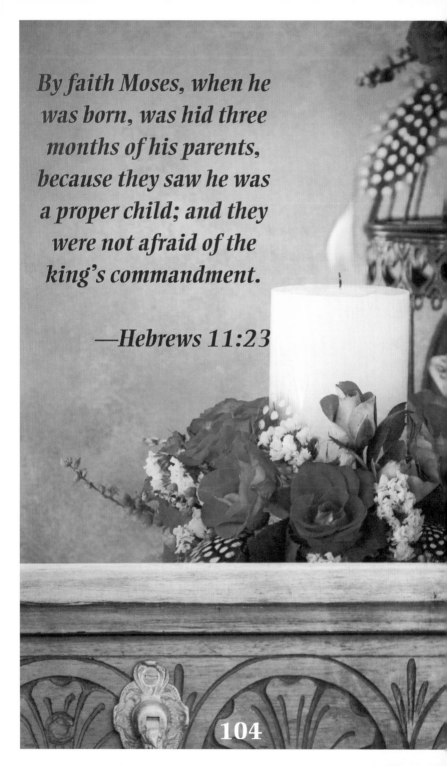

*By faith Moses, when he
was born, was hid three
months of his parents,
because they saw he was
a proper child; and they
were not afraid of the
king's commandment.*

—Hebrews 11:23

Dear Lord, my role as a mother puts me in a commanding position. Children have little power, and it is up to me, as my child's mother, to be a helpmeet and advocate in a world that is not always just. My son, who is nine, has been dealing with a bully at school. I've had to go in to meet with the principal and the other boy's parents several times, and the parents have on more than one occasion grown belligerent. It's an uncomfortable situation, but I know I must remain strong and levelheaded in order to support my child. God, please grant me the strength to always do what is right for my child, even at risk of personal discomfort, as the parents of Moses did.

Therefore shall a man leave his father and his mother, and shall cleave unto his wife: and they shall be one flesh.

—Genesis 2:24

Love is a challenge. Marriage is an even bigger one. Being a good wife often means compromising with my spouse and finding the balance in our relationship. I can get selfish and want what I want, but a true partnership strives to satisfy the needs of both, not just one. Marriage often means thinking in terms of the unit, not just the individuals. God, may you always be present in my marriage, guiding me and encouraging me to be the best wife I can be to my husband. I ask you, God, to empower me with the wisdom, patience, and understanding that makes a partnership a happy one for both parties involved. May I always focus on the bigger unit we chose when we said "I do."

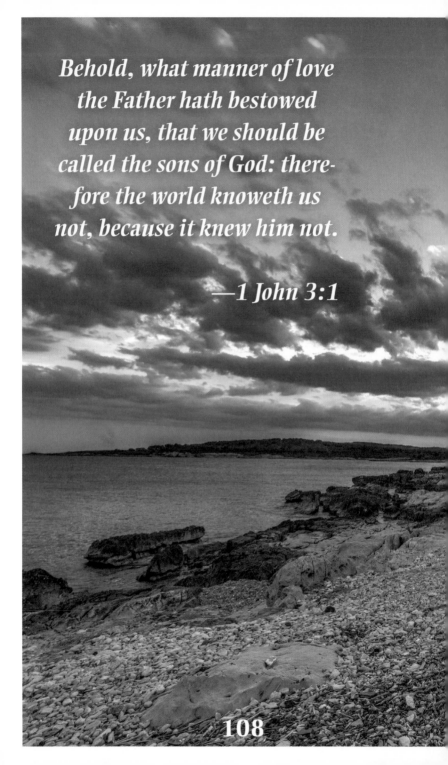

Behold, what manner of love the Father hath bestowed upon us, that we should be called the sons of God: therefore the world knoweth us not, because it knew him not.

—1 John 3:1

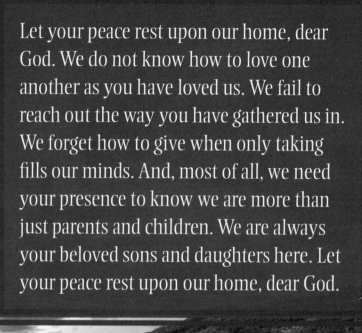

Let your peace rest upon our home, dear God. We do not know how to love one another as you have loved us. We fail to reach out the way you have gathered us in. We forget how to give when only taking fills our minds. And, most of all, we need your presence to know we are more than just parents and children. We are always your beloved sons and daughters here. Let your peace rest upon our home, dear God.

Lo, children are an heritage of the Lord: and the fruit of the womb is his reward.

—Psalm 127:3

Father, you have enriched my life with many identities—daughter, student, wife, and mother. Richness and joy have followed me through each phase of my life, and I have wholeheartedly accepted and enjoyed each role. But you knew, didn't you, Lord, that the title of mother would make such a strong claim on my heart? How I praise you for the greatest of your gifts, my children, and for the fulfillment they have brought. I need no other affirmation than to be called mother. My children have taught me to forget myself, and through them, I have learned what it means to be your child.

My husband and I have three children under the age of ten. We love being parents, even as we understand that parenting can entail sacrifice. This came home to us recently when my husband declined an opportunity for promotion. Though the job sounded interesting, it meant that he would be traveling three weeks out of every four. We have decided our priority, right now, is for both of us to hold jobs where we can be consistently home and together as a family. The job offer was good, but the timing was not. Though these decisions can be difficult, God reminds us to sacrifice happily for our children. If we sometimes have to defer our own gratification, seeing our children thrive is a blessing.

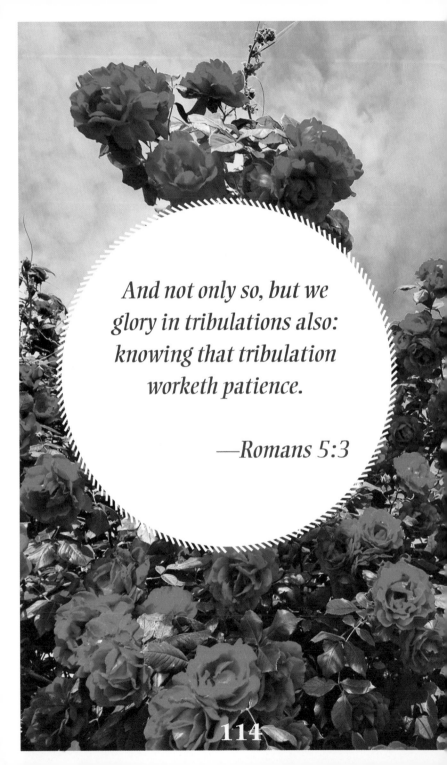

And not only so, but we glory in tribulations also: knowing that tribulation worketh patience.

—Romans 5:3

As a parent, what I wish for my daughter Anne is an easy path. When she struggles with her studies or experiences conflicts with friends, my heart aches. I know, however, that no one can be shielded from pain indefinitely, and that it is adversity as well as our joys and successes that shape us. My grandfather used to say that misfortune can build character, and I see that in my daughter: challenges have shown her that she possesses an inner steel, even as they've demanded she develop patience and compassion. Dear Lord, help me to guide Anne so that she might meet hardship with strength, patience, and grace. May adversity help her to grow as a person.

Every man according as he purposeth in his heart, so let him give; not grudgingly, or of necessity: for God loveth a cheerful giver.

—2 Corinthians 9:7

My husband is a nurse, and lately the hospital where he works has been short-staffed. Though new hires will soon be brought onboard, for the time being, my husband's schedule is more taxing. When I promised him I would pick up more of the slack at home, I was sincere. And yet, yesterday I was tired and ungraciously reminded my husband of all I was doing. His face fell, and I was ashamed; here we are, both working so hard, and I spoiled my kind efforts with bitterness! I have since made amends, but dear Lord, please remind me to give with good cheer, not grumbling.

And Ruth said, Intreat me not to leave thee, or to return from following after thee: for whither thou goest, I will go; and where thou lodgest, I will lodge: thy people shall be my people, and thy God my God.

—Ruth 1:16

Children have the most amazing capacity for loyalty, God; they look to their parents with trust that all will be well. Sometimes I fear that I cannot live up to the faith that my children put in me, that I am not as strong or as invincible as they believe me to be. Lord, help me appreciate their trust as the privilege that it is. Help me to be a rock for my young ones, even as you are a rock for me. You see into my heart; you know the strength and fear that exist side by side within it. May you guide me— helping me access the strength I possess and the strength you give freely—as I strive to create a stable and loving home life for my family.

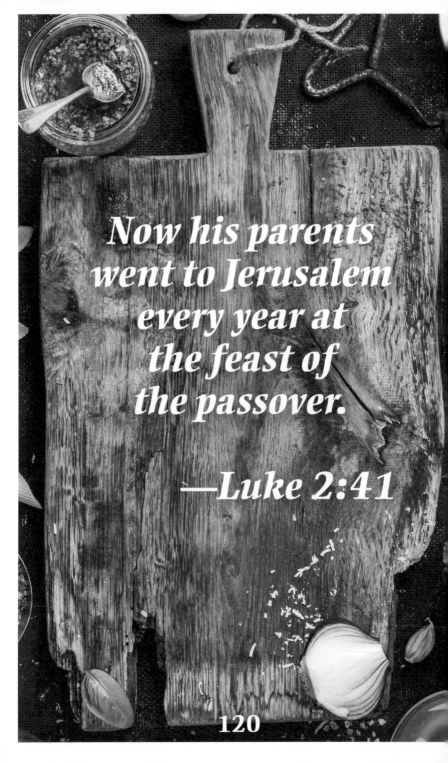

*Now his parents
went to Jerusalem
every year at
the feast of
the passover.*

—Luke 2:41

My husband, two children, and I recently took a road trip to Boston. My middle school son has been studying the American Revolution, and Boston's rich history and wealth of museums drew us. We had a wonderful time exploring the city, but an unanticipated pleasure was the time it took to drive from our Midwestern home to the East Coast and back again. In the car, we read, talked, and listened to music. Upon our return home, we felt refreshed and connected, and my son mentioned that the next time we travel, he hopes we drive again. As he put it: "It'll be our tradition, you know?" The next day we went to church together, and I felt that same connection. Lord, I am reminded of the importance of family traditions—like going on road trips or worshipping together—and the bonds and continuity they foster. Please grant me the creativity to pursue traditions that enrich my family life; may I never lose sight of their importance.

And Jesus said unto them,
I am the bread of life: he
that cometh to me shall
never hunger; and he
that believeth on me shall
never thirst.

—John 6:35

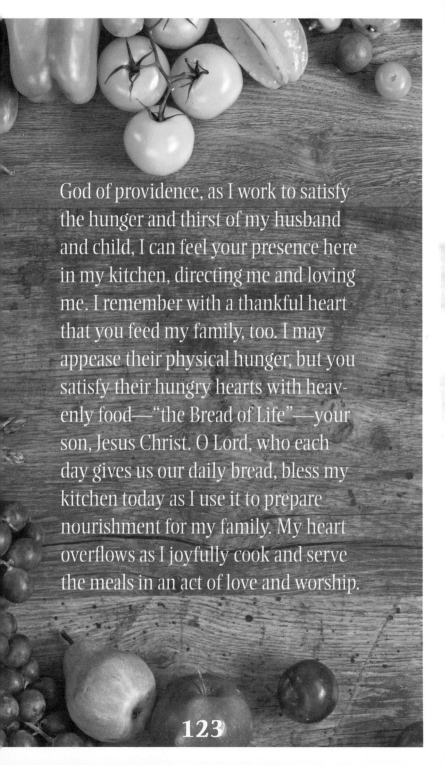

God of providence, as I work to satisfy the hunger and thirst of my husband and child, I can feel your presence here in my kitchen, directing me and loving me. I remember with a thankful heart that you feed my family, too. I may appease their physical hunger, but you satisfy their hungry hearts with heavenly food—"the Bread of Life"—your son, Jesus Christ. O Lord, who each day gives us our daily bread, bless my kitchen today as I use it to prepare nourishment for my family. My heart overflows as I joyfully cook and serve the meals in an act of love and worship.

Her children arise up, and call her blessed;
her husband also, and he praiseth her.

—Proverbs 31:28

This morning there were, as my grandfather used to say, a lot of moving parts. My husband needed to catch an early train into the city, my son Ben couldn't find his chemistry textbook, and our dog scarfed down the bread I'd intended for everyone's lunch sandwiches. I was feeling pretty frazzled, and had to get to work myself. But after the boys got out the door and I'd made sure the dog was none the worse for wear, I took a deep breath and noticed that Ben had made me a pot of coffee before leaving for school. My husband had promised he'd order us a pizza tonight so that no one had to cook. And our dog? Well, it's hard to stay mad at a smiling dog! Lord, even when things are a little crazy around our house, I thank you: I am blessed by my family.

Talk no more so exceeding proudly;
let not arrogancy come out of your mouth:
for the Lord is a God of knowledge,
and by him actions are weighed.

—1 Samuel 2:3

Lord, nothing is more humbling than the loved ones who've known me for my whole life. When I catch up with my siblings and cousins, we are anchored by memories of silly childhood choices and even serious adult mistakes. What a blessing it is to have people in my life with whom I share so much history and so many special memories; who forgive me and see the whole person I am.

What therefore God hath joined together, let not man put asunder.

—Mark 10:9

My husband and I have encountered a rough patch in our marriage. Our youngest child recently began college, and transitioning to an "empty nest" home has been harder on us both than we anticipated. My husband, who misses our sons, has started a new job. He's not home as much just as I've begun contemplating taking early retirement. So many days we seem to be at cross-purposes—we seem to want different things! But this morning when we sat down together over coffee, my husband reminded me that over the years, we have weathered many storms in our marriage—job loss, the deaths of our parents, our middle son's struggles with schoolwork and drugs. Each time we have prevailed together. It was a good conversation, and I think we felt closer to one another than we have in months. Dear Lord, you have joined my husband and me. You have blessed our partnership. To succeed, we must take the long view!

Ye shall not respect persons in judgment;
but ye shall hear the small as well as the
great; ye shall not be afraid of the face of
man; for the judgment is God's.

—*Deuteronomy 1:17*

Lord, today I slighted one of my children without meaning to. I didn't listen when he offered his opinion, and he wondered if I dismissed him as being "just a kid." Everyone is special and everyone has valid input to offer. It's my responsibility to raise my children to be confident, thoughtful people. My son forgave me with great poise—I am as proud of him as I am embarrassed for myself. Thank you, God, for the blessing of his sweet personality and growing presence of mind.

And the Lord God said, It is not good that the man should be alone; I will make him an help meet for him.

—Genesis 2:18

My husband and I have been married for 25 years. Around the time, we celebrated that milestone anniversary; we each began to pursue self-employment ventures that allow us to work from home. Several friends have laughingly asked if we get on one another's nerves, but working from home has actually been a real joy for us both. We like working together in the living room with music playing in the background. We both love the company of our cats. I really enjoy that my husband and I can eat lunch together, and sometimes we'll take a break in the afternoon and swim laps at the Y. My husband is my best friend. God, thank you for the everyday companionship that a strong marriage brings.

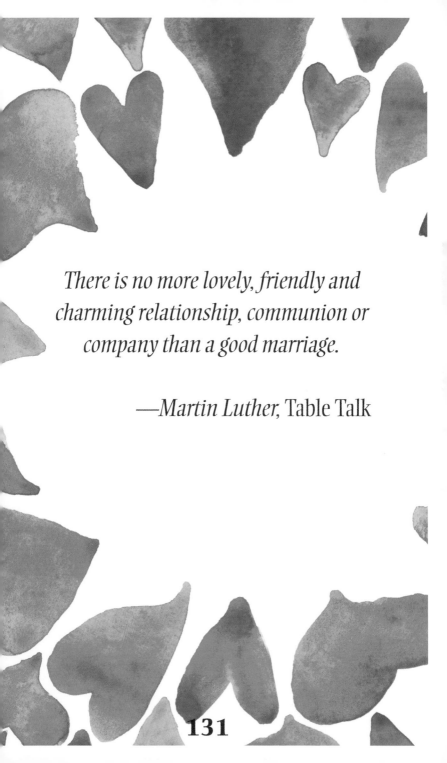

There is no more lovely, friendly and charming relationship, communion or company than a good marriage.

—*Martin Luther,* Table Talk

A soft answer turneth away wrath:
but grievous words stir up anger.

—Proverbs 15:1

My sister Emma and I are like night and day: even though we grew up in the same house, and were raised by the same parents, our worldviews are strikingly different. We've had different ideas about how to help our aging parents, and we have different ideas on how to be a parent. And though we love each other, we don't always get along. Yesterday Emma criticized the way I'm handling a conflict with a mutual friend, and I had to bite my tongue to keep from lashing out. I managed to respond with a joke, and it was amazing, how the tension between us drained away. God, help me to remember: when in a quarrel, I must strive to take the high road. A soft answer can defuse an argument before it begins.

He that spareth his rod hateth his son: but he that loveth him chasteneth him betimes.

—Proverbs 13:24

My son doesn't like doing homework. It's hard for him—he struggles with academics and he'd rather be playing baseball, a sport at which he excels. God, I don't like conflict. I want to be my son's friend. And we can butt heads when I insist he complete his work before play: I have lost my temper on more than one occasion, frustrated because he needs to do the work and yet doesn't want to do the work. Frustrated because I don't like to fight with him. Sometimes I am tired and tempted to just let it go, though I know this would do him no favors. Dear God, help me to step up to the plate and be the adult I need to be. Please give me the strength to discipline my children when necessary, and help me to do so with love.

And above all things have fervent charity among yourselves: for charity shall cover the multitude of sins.

—1 Peter 4:8

My husband and I are newly married, and we have encountered some growing pains as we adjust to sharing a home and making a life together. One persistent source of discord is the fact that I am something of a neatnik, while my husband is more relaxed about keeping our apartment tidy. I can see that he tries, but it still drives me a little crazy when he leaves dirty dishes on the counter, or toothpaste spatters in the sink. These are such little things, but sometimes they get to me, and I said as much to my mother the last time we were together. Mom has been married to my dad for more than 30 years, and she responded to me with gentle humor: "Choose your battles and remember: love helps us overlook one another's flaws." My parents have an extraordinarily loving marriage, and Mom's words have stayed with me. Dear Lord, please help me remember that love is the root of a strong marriage, and that love helps us accept our partners as they are, warts and all.

Open thy mouth for the dumb in the cause of all such as are appointed to destruction.

—Proverbs 31:8

Lynne's six-year-old daughter Phoebe has a severe peanut allergy, but the school Phoebe attends did not have any protocols in place should the girl experience an allergic reaction. At first, the school administration did not appreciate the severity of Phoebe's allergy, which is in fact life threatening. Lynne's initial efforts to bring attention to her daughter's condition were treated dismissively; she had to dig deep to be the firm, wise advocate her daughter's situation demanded. Dear Lord, please help me to be ready to speak up for those who cannot speak for themselves. May I be a wise and thoughtful advocate.

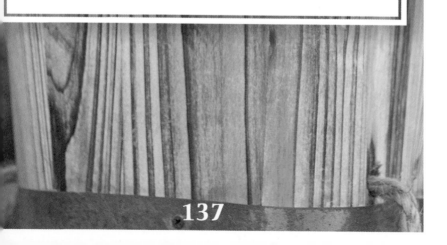

GRATITUDE

To the end that my glory may sing praise to thee, and not be silent. O Lord my God, I will give thanks unto thee for ever.

—Psalm 30:12

Lord, please help me to be more focused on the good in life and less focused on the bad. I know that faith is what brings good things into my world, but sometimes my faith gets a little shaky and I end up dwelling on the bad stuff going on around me. Show me how to open my heart back up and see things with new eyes. Change my perspective so that I can understand on a deeper level that what is happening to me is a blessing and not a curse. For this I am grateful, Lord.

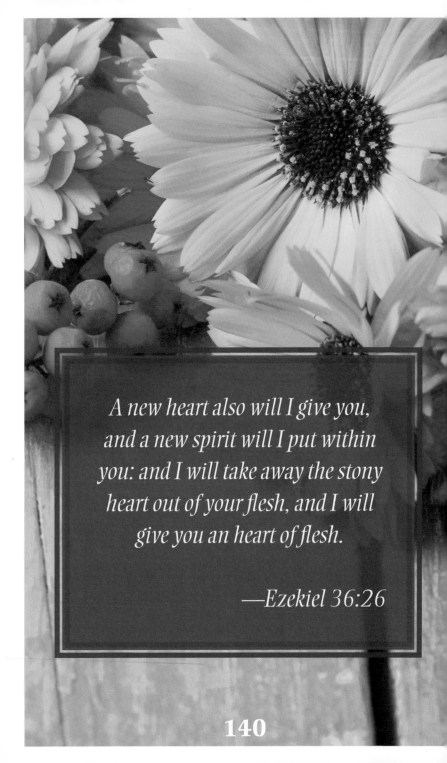

A new heart also will I give you, and a new spirit will I put within you: and I will take away the stony heart out of your flesh, and I will give you an heart of flesh.

—Ezekiel 36:26

Today, Lord, I want to be guided by a grateful heart. As I understand it, a grateful heart doesn't search for what's missing but delights in what's present. A grateful heart expects the best from others and gives its best in return. A grateful heart forgets what might have been and enjoys every moment of each new day as it comes. A grateful heart is a prayer of its own—one that fills the heavens with praise! Please, Lord, give me a grateful heart.

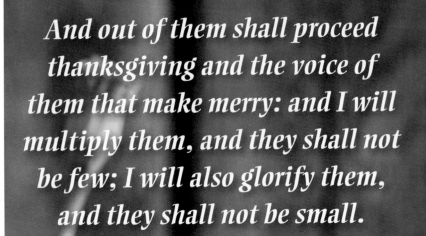

And out of them shall proceed thanksgiving and the voice of them that make merry: and I will multiply them, and they shall not be few; I will also glorify them, and they shall not be small.

—Jeremiah 30:19

Dear Lord, I thank you for the wonderful things with which you have filled my life. I have family and friends who care, clothing to wear, food to eat, and shelter over my head. You have not only provided for me, but bountifully so. I do have my challenges, but I always stop and reflect on the ways you've blessed me, and lo and behold, I am blessed with even more to enjoy and share with others. How awesome is it to watch blessings multiply? How amazing is it to see how you magnify my good to the point of overflowing? My heart is filled with such gratitude, Lord, for your grace and glory!

Take heed therefore unto yourselves, and to all the flock, over the which the Holy Ghost hath made you overseers, to feed the church of God, which he hath purchased with his own blood.

—Acts 20:28

Lord, today my heart is full of gratitude for your church. Thank you for asking us to meet together to honor you. What power there is in voicing our thanks and petitions together! What comfort in the outstretched arms of friends! Protect us, Lord. Keep us strong—now and in the days to come.

And he shall be as the light of the morning, when the sun riseth, even a morning without clouds; as the tender grass springing out of the earth by clear shining after rain.

—2 Samuel 23:4

With boldness, wonder, and expectation, I greet you this morning, God of sunrise and rising dew. Gratefully, I look back to all that was good yesterday and in hope, face forward, ready for today.

Wherefore comfort yourselves together, and edify one another, even as also ye do.

—1 Thessalonians 5:11

Bless those who mentor, model, and cheer me on, Lord, urging me toward goals I set, applauding as I reach them, and nourishing me to try again when I don't. Remind me to be a cheerleader. I plan to say thanks to those who are mine.

*For the administration of
this service not only supplieth the
want of the saints, but is abundant
also by many thanksgivings unto God.*

—2 Corinthians 9:12

Thank you, God, for the salesclerk who
took an extra moment to be gracious,
for the person who delivered my mail,
and for the drivers who yielded to me
without hesitation. I do not know their
names, but they blessed me today with
their hard work and positive attitudes.

O give thanks unto the Lord; for he is good; for his mercy endureth for ever.

—1 Chronicles 16:34

Gratitude may the most highly underestimated virtue. We think of love, hope, faith, and the power of prayer and forgiveness. But how often do we stop each day and give thanks for all the blessings in our lives? Are we too focused on what we lack, what we don't have, don't want, don't need? By opening the heart and mind to focus on gratitude, we unleash a treasure of unceasing good that's just waiting to overflow into our lives. A grateful person knows that by giving thanks, they're given even more to be thankful for.

Honour the Lord with thy substance, and with the first-fruits of all thine increase.

—Proverbs 3:9

150

Dear Lord, I am blessed. Life can be difficult but it is also beautiful, and I am thankful that my husband and I have work even in difficult times. Our family has enough to eat; my children have friends who are good to them; we are healthy. In fact, good health gives me the energy to parent my children, to do the work I need to do, to support others—and indeed, God, what are we here for if not to connect with and uplift those around us?—and to pursue passions that fulfill me. Yesterday I worked in the garden. The peppers are blooming and my cat dozed in the shade nearby. My heart was so full! God, thank you. Please help me to remember gratitude, and may I always remember to honor you with everything I have.

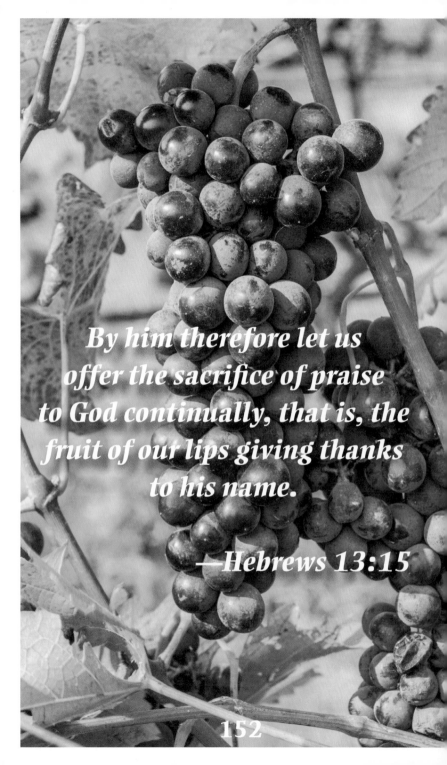

By him therefore let us offer the sacrifice of praise to God continually, that is, the fruit of our lips giving thanks to his name.

—Hebrews 13:15

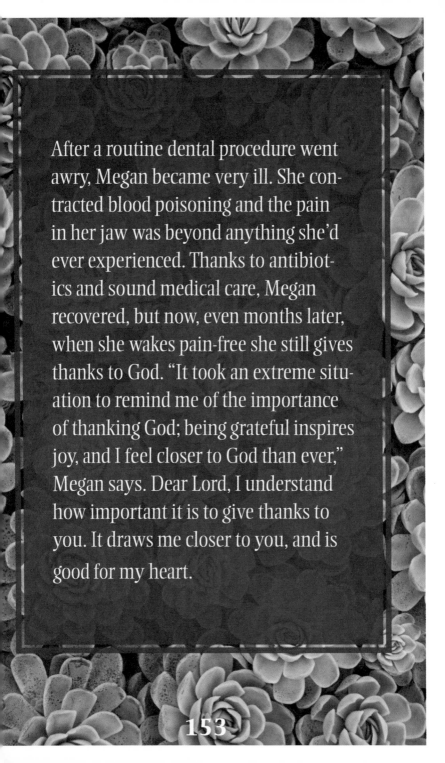

After a routine dental procedure went awry, Megan became very ill. She contracted blood poisoning and the pain in her jaw was beyond anything she'd ever experienced. Thanks to antibiotics and sound medical care, Megan recovered, but now, even months later, when she wakes pain-free she still gives thanks to God. "It took an extreme situation to remind me of the importance of thanking God; being grateful inspires joy, and I feel closer to God than ever," Megan says. Dear Lord, I understand how important it is to give thanks to you. It draws me closer to you, and is good for my heart.

That the trial of your faith, being much more precious than of gold that perisheth, though it be tried with fire, might be found unto praise and honour and glory at the appearing of Jesus Christ.

—1 Peter 1:7

It's so easy to be thankful for the good. But when we encounter obstacles, how often do we curse them? Yet those difficulties are helping us to evolve into better and stronger and more loving human beings. It's easy to be grateful once the challenges are gone and we are once again in the flow of life. But try to be grateful for the hard times as well. They are very often miracles in disguise.

O Lord, we give thanks for your presence, which greets us each day in the guise of a friend, a work of nature, or a story from a stranger. We are reminded through these messengers in our times of deepest need that you are indeed watching over us. Lord, we have known you in the love and care of a friend, who envelops and keeps us company in our despair. When we observe the last morning glory stretching faithfully to receive what warmth is left in the chilly sunshine, we are heartened and inspired to do the same. When we are hesitant to speak up and then read in the newspaper a story of courage and controversy, we find our voice lifted and strengthened by your message in black-and-white type. Lord, we are grateful receivers of all the angelic messages that surround us every day.

Teach me, Lord, to look at the world with hope and expectation, not with despair and lack. I am grateful for all you have done for me, but there is still this emptiness inside that catches up to me now and then. Help me see how wonderful my life is, just as it is, and that nothing more is needed to be happy and at peace, for those are gifts that come from within. Teach me to keep my eyes on the bounty that comes from a thankful heart, not from the things we acquire but from the experiences we have and the love we give. Amen.

I never realized the power of making a gratitude list when nothing was going right. With financial stresses and my son suffering from health issues, it seemed there was little I could put on that list. But every night before I went to sleep, I forced myself to write down five good things that had happened that day. Sometimes they were small things, and inconsequential to anyone but me. But soon my lists were well over five. My lists today often surpass 20 things to be grateful for.

It is a good thing to give thanks unto the Lord, and to sing praises unto thy name, O Most High.

—Psalm 92:1

Each day brings new things to be happy about, God, and I am really loving my life for the first time in a long time. I am so grateful for this new way of looking at things, seeing the glass half full instead of empty, and always looking for the bright side of the coin. Your blessings are everywhere, but it took me awhile to notice them because I was so caught up in the stress and strain of my daily life. Thank you for opening my eyes to a whole new world of wonder and joy.

*The Lord shall preserve thy going out
and thy coming in from this time forth,
and even for evermore.*

—Psalm 121:8

I recently retired after almost 40 years of teaching. As much as I enjoyed my job, I am reveling in the opportunities this new chapter affords. I have always loved travel, and for many years dreamed of visiting Europe; my gift to myself this next year is a month-long tour through France and Italy. While I am excited, I am also a little anxious: I'll be traveling solo, and have never been away from home for so long. Dear God, thank you for this opportunity. Please bless my travels. Please guide and protect me as I visit new places, meet new people, and broaden my horizons. May I make the most of this journey.

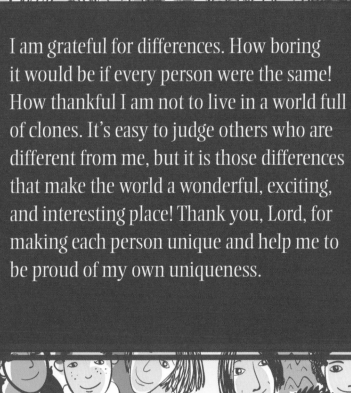

I am grateful for differences. How boring it would be if every person were the same! How thankful I am not to live in a world full of clones. It's easy to judge others who are different from me, but it is those differences that make the world a wonderful, exciting, and interesting place! Thank you, Lord, for making each person unique and help me to be proud of my own uniqueness.

Delight thyself also in the Lord; and he shall give thee the desires of thine heart.
—Psalm 37:4

Ever notice how thinking about what you are grateful for often leads to more things to be grateful for? When our hearts and eyes are focused on the amazing good God has given us, we realize we have little need for anything else. And yet...he gives us more. We can go to God in prayer and he answers, giving us the deepest yearnings of our hearts. It all starts with turning to God in the first place, and not to the ways and things of the world. Start with God, and we end up with all we've ever hoped and dreamed of. Thank you, God, for fulfilling my deepest desires with your everlasting presence and love. Thank you for knowing my heart even better than I know it myself.

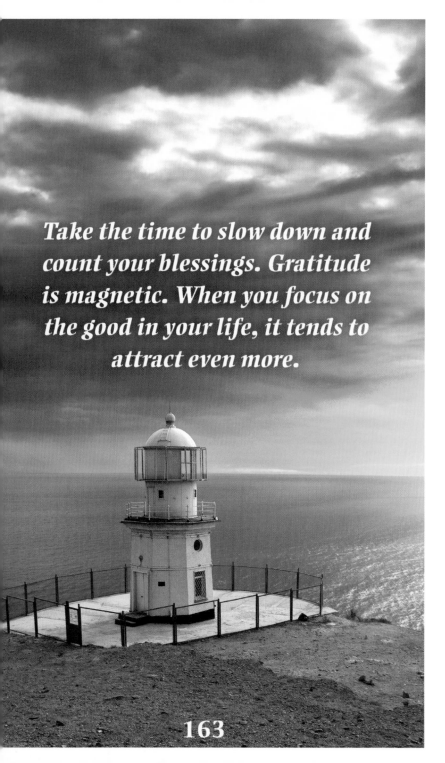

Take the time to slow down and count your blessings. Gratitude is magnetic. When you focus on the good in your life, it tends to attract even more.

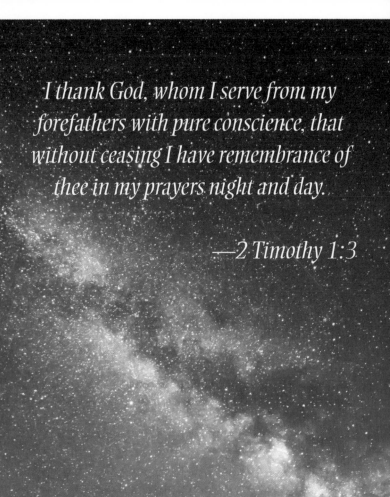

I thank God, whom I serve from my forefathers with pure conscience, that without ceasing I have remembrance of thee in my prayers night and day.

—2 Timothy 1:3

164

Lord, we are so thankful to you for our families and close friends. How lonely our lives would be without them, even in this splendid world of your making! What a privilege it is to come to you every day to offer prayers for them. Day after day I bring before you those close to me who need your special attention. If I can't sleep at night, I pray for them again. Each one is so precious to me, Lord, and I know you cherish them as well. As I think of them during the day, please consider each thought to be another small prayer.

And I will bring the blind by a way that they knew not; I will lead them in paths that they have not known: I will make darkness light before them, and crooked things straight. These things will I do unto them, and not forsake them.

—Isaiah 42:16

Lord, how grateful I am that you are willing to go before me to prepare the way. Even when I sense that a new opportunity is from you and has your blessing, I've learned I still need to stop and ask you to lead before I take the first step. Otherwise I will stumble along in the dark tripping over stones of my own creation! Everything goes more smoothly when you are involved, Lord.

Where would we be without our elders? When I think about the people who came before me, I am filled with gratitude for their hard work and sacrifices. It is good to remember what they did and how they lived. Thank you, Lord, for giving us strong forebearers who shaped the world and always looked toward creating a better future. Without them, my life would be very different. Help me appreciate and value the past.

Lord, my heart overflows with gratitude for all the blessings you have sent into my life. I am cognizant of the fact that I am probably only aware of a small percentage of them, though. You are such a generous God; you shower us with such abundance. I am grateful for it all, Lord.

Gratitude is an attitude of loving what you have, and this undoubtedly leads to having even more. When you open your eyes to the bountiful blessings already in your life, you realize just how abundant the world really is. Suddenly, you feel more giving, more loving, and more open to even greater blessings. Gratitude is a key that unlocks the door to treasures you already have, and it yields greater treasures yet to be discovered.

These things I have spoken unto you, that in me ye might have peace. In the world ye shall have tribulation: but be of good cheer; I have overcome the world.

—John 16:33

Lord, how easy it is to express gratitude when times are good, but how difficult it can be for us to also thank you for the hard times—especially when we are in the midst of them. That's not wise of us, Lord, and we are sorry. For when we look back over all the ups and downs of our lives, we see that you were in fact working all things together for good. For lessons learned in the hard times, and for the strength you gave us to get through them, we give you thanks. After all, how can we not be grateful for anything that brings us closer to you? So thank you, Lord, even for the hard times.

FORGIVENESS

Thus saith the Lord of hosts;
Consider your ways.

—Haggai 1:7

Gently, Lord, love me gently on this tough day. I'm hurting now because of my own mistake. It's nothing serious, but it especially hurts to know I brought the pain upon myself and disappointed you. The silver lining is that I know how to resolve the situation. Lord, I love that your Word and my own feelings coincide when it comes to knowing right from wrong, even if I sometimes ignore my better judgment. Thank you for welcoming me back into the fold every time without fail.

As far as the east is from the west,
so far hath he removed our
transgressions from us.

—Psalm 103:12

O Lord, when you promise us you
have removed our sins from us, why
do we dredge them up so we can
wallow in regret and shame all over
again? Keep us from wasting time and
energy thinking about past mistakes,
Lord. If they are no longer on your
radar, they surely don't belong on
ours. How blessed we are to have
such a compassionate, forgiving God!

*And when ye
stand praying, forgive,
if ye have ought against any:
that your Father also which
is in heaven may forgive you
your trespasses.*

—Mark 11:25

Father, I need to understand that forgiveness is not dependent on my feelings, but rather on a determination of my will. Help me form a few well-chosen words of forgiveness. Amen.

Be ye angry, and sin not: let not the sun go down upon your wrath: Neither give place to the devil.

—Ephesians 4:26–27

Heavenly Father, teach me to forgive others their transgressions and to let go of angers and resentments that poison the heart and burden the soul. Teach me to love and understand others and to accept them as they are, not as I wish they would be. Amen.

If we confess our sins, he is faithful and just to forgive us our sins, and to cleanse us from all unrighteousness.

—1 John 1:9

God, I am not perfect. I continue to sin and make mistakes. Sometimes I do things that I am not proud of or that bring me nothing but a sense of shame and guilt, even though I know better at the time. I often make lousy decisions. I know it is human nature, but I aspire to be more like you in all my ways. It helps me to know that you forgive me my shortcomings, but I still pray for the wisdom, strength, and fortitude to stop having so many short-comings to forgive. I understand life is about progress, not perfection, God. May I always do better, but when I fall short, thank you for forgiving me.

177

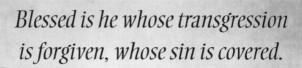

Blessed is he whose transgression is forgiven, whose sin is covered.

—Psalm 32:1

My Lord, this world continues to have an obsession with happiness. Ads proclaim that we can't be happy without this product or that service, and so we add to the long list of things that may please us for a while, but can't deliver true happiness. Forgive our fruitless chasing after happiness, Lord, for we know that it can only exist in relationship with you. Until we know you and seek your forgiveness, we can't know happiness. But with you, we are full of joy!

O Lord, your willingness to forgive is astounding! You've never done anything wrong, and yet you are ready to forgive those who have sinned against you whenever they sincerely confess and turn away from the wrong they've done. I want to thank you for being so merciful toward me, for forgiving my debt of sin. I will always praise you for your goodness in dealing with me so gently. Help me to remember to be merciful toward others, just as you have been toward me.

The greatest gift we can offer someone is our forgiveness, for it has the dual power to set the other person free and to set us free as well.

Holy God, I am praying for forgiveness—not from you, but from the one I hurt. I acted thoughtlessly, perhaps even maliciously, and I have harmed that person. I have already received your forgiveness by coming to you in penitence, but I need to seek forgiveness from the one I hurt, and I am afraid he will not accept my apology. I ask for strength to admit my wrongdoing to him, and I ask that you will soften his heart toward me. I know I was wrong. I do not deserve forgiveness, but I pray that he will have mercy on me as you have. Amen.

Let all bitterness, and wrath, and anger, and clamour, and evil speaking, be put away from you, with all malice: And be ye kind one to another, tenderhearted, forgiving one another, even as God for Christ's sake hath forgiven you.

—*Ephesians 4:31–32*

My supreme Lord, give me a forgiving heart. When someone unintentionally ignores me or hurts my feelings, let me respond with forgiveness before they are even aware of the wrong. In these and other situations, I pray that forgiveness will become an automatic response for me and not something I have to consciously work on. I guess what I'm really asking, Lord, is please give me a heart like yours. Only then will I be able to live a life full of spontaneous forgiveness.

In whom we have redemption through his blood, the forgiveness of sins, according to the riches of his grace.

—Ephesians 1:7

Dear Jesus, you have given us the greatest gift imaginable through your birth and death—the gift of salvation. You have rescued us from despair and hopelessness by dying to atone for our sins. The forgiveness you have brought to our lives is the most precious gift we could ever hope for. Today, let me revel in the glory of redemption and know that I am saved, for this world and for all eternity. Amen.

And they shall teach no more every man his neighbour, and every man his brother, saying, Know the Lord: for they shall all know me, from the least of them unto the greatest of them, saith the Lord: for I will forgive their iniquity, and I will remember their sin no more.

—*Jeremiah 31:34*

I am not sure, heavenly Father, that I can ever forget this pain. I know that time will heal all wounds, and that one day I will look back on this as a lesson learned and wisdom gained. But right now, I struggle to keep from letting anger and depression overcome me. Help me find that middle road, where I can forgive, even if I am not yet able to forget. I long to be free of the dark fog that envelops me, and I pray that you will embolden me to step forward and move beyond what was done to me to the hope of what will be. Amen.

Forgiveness is the central virtue in God's treasure chest—God's forgiveness of us and our forgiveness of others and ourselves. At times we find that forgiveness comes very easily, even for grievous and painful hurts. But many times, we seem powerless to forgive, no matter how hard we try. This is when God's forgiving grace has the opportunity to touch and change us and then be extended to others through our example.

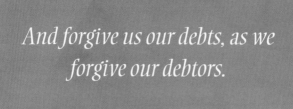

And forgive us our debts, as we forgive our debtors.

—Matthew 6:12

Lord God, the words "I'm sorry" and "forgive me" have got to be the most powerful in our vocabulary. May these phrases ever be poised on my lips, ready to do their work of release and restoration. Let your healing balm wash over me, Father, as I both grant and receive the freedom that forgiveness brings. Amen.

Wherefore I say unto thee, Her sins, which are many, are forgiven; for she loved much: but to whom little is forgiven, the same loveth little.

—Luke 7:47

Lord, it is tempting and easy to cast a scornful eye on those around us and note every fault. When my pride tempts me to do so, prompt me to turn the magnifying glass on myself instead. If I keep in mind how much I need your forgiveness every day, my love for you will never grow cold. I know you are willing to forgive each and every fault if I only ask.

To him give all the prophets witness, that through his name whosoever believeth in him shall receive remission of sins.

—Acts 10:43

What does redemption mean? To me, it means to be cleansed and renewed, free from the burdens of my past mistakes. God, your forgiveness brings me that clarity and redemption, and that renewal of my spirit. Your grace frees me from the bonds of the past that weighed me down and made my life feel so heavy. I ask in prayer today that you work with me to free those who I've kept in the bondage of their sins against me. Help me forgive them, not just because it will set me free of anger and pain in the process, but also because you have already forgiven them. We all sin. We all deserve to be made clean and whole again.

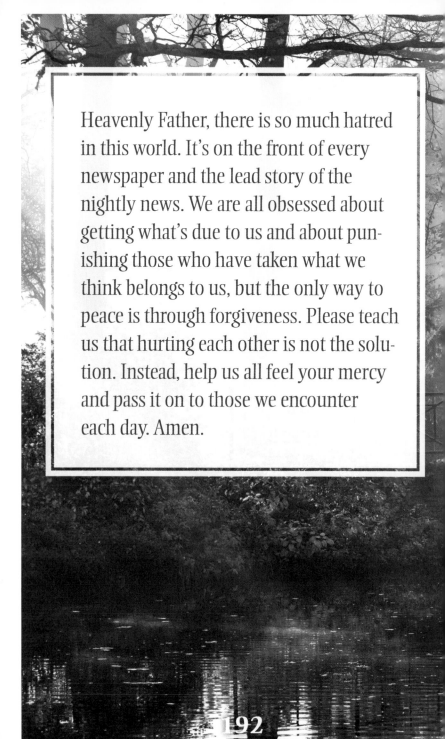

Heavenly Father, there is so much hatred in this world. It's on the front of every newspaper and the lead story of the nightly news. We are all obsessed about getting what's due to us and about punishing those who have taken what we think belongs to us, but the only way to peace is through forgiveness. Please teach us that hurting each other is not the solution. Instead, help us all feel your mercy and pass it on to those we encounter each day. Amen.

God, why is it so difficult to forgive the people who are closest to me? I feel that they should love me enough to never hurt me, yet they do so many times. Since I don't want to be bitter and resentful, help me find the courage to forgive their pettiness and see beyond the smallness of their behavior. I know I am not always perfect either, and I pray they may also forgive me for hurting them, too. We always seem to hurt the ones we love, but teach me, God, how to forgive and be forgiven. Amen.

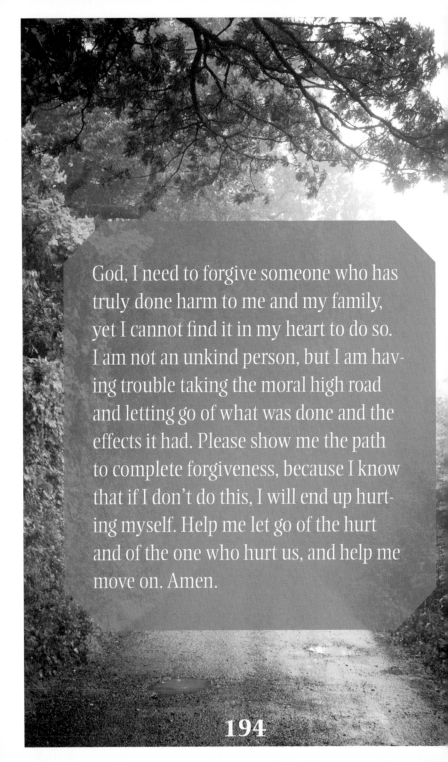

God, I need to forgive someone who has truly done harm to me and my family, yet I cannot find it in my heart to do so. I am not an unkind person, but I am having trouble taking the moral high road and letting go of what was done and the effects it had. Please show me the path to complete forgiveness, because I know that if I don't do this, I will end up hurting myself. Help me let go of the hurt and of the one who hurt us, and help me move on. Amen.

I blew it. Give me courage to admit my mistake, apologize, and go on. Keep me from getting stuck in denial, despair, and, worst of all, fear of trying again. In your remolding hands, God of grace, failures can become feedback and mistakes can simply be lessons in what doesn't work. Remind me that perfection means "suited to the task," not "without mistakes." There's a world of difference.

I acknowledge my sin unto thee, and mine iniquity have I not hid. I said, I will confess my transgressions unto the Lord; and thou forgavest the iniquity of my sin.

—Psalm 32:5

Lord, you forgive us all our transgressions, and for that I am grateful. Though I strive to always do the right thing, I know that my sins will be forgiven if they are made with a heart willing to learn and to grow. By forgiving me, you free me to be who I am, warts and all, always knowing that I am loved no matter how I mess up. I aspire to be perfect in your eyes, Lord, but it is good to know that if I fall short now and then, all is forgiven.

My Lord, you instructed us to forgive our enemies, but I need a little extra courage to do that today. I want to hold on to my anger like a weapon, but in my heart I know that I am just hurting myself by doing so. I pray for some strength and fortitude to face my responsibilities for what happened and to accept what others did in kind. I pray to forgive those who have betrayed me, even as I ask them to forgive me for my role in this situation. Help me, Lord, to forgive them.

Have mercy upon me, O God, according to thy lovingkindness: according unto the multitude of thy tender mercies blot out my transgressions. Wash me throughly from mine iniquity, and cleanse me from my sin. For I acknowledge my transgressions: and my sin is ever before me.

—Psalm 51:1–3

Help me, God, to see that you gave your love in such a way that even the most wicked person can repent and find new life in your grace and mercy; indeed, that your love calls even the worst sinners to become your children. You created each person with a specific purpose to serve in this world. Help me, Lord, to pray that each person will turn away from evil, turn to you, and become your devoted servant. Amen.

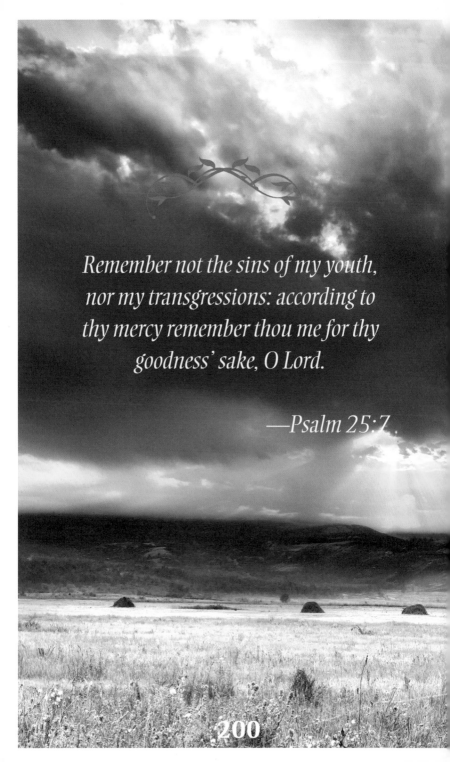

Remember not the sins of my youth, nor my transgressions: according to thy mercy remember thou me for thy goodness' sake, O Lord.

—Psalm 25:7

Sometimes, Father, the shame and pain of past regrets can ambush my thoughts and emotions. When that happens, it doesn't take long for me to turn against myself with feelings of self-loathing and anger. The next step in my downward spiral is that I start lashing out at those around me—especially those closest to me. Oh, Father! How futile that sequence of turmoil is when you've fully forgiven me for my past transgressions! Please halt me when I begin to revisit what you have chosen to wash away. Help me look myself in the eye and say, "Your heavenly Father loves you and has forgiven you. You are forgiven. Now it's time to forgive yourself and live as one set free." Thank you for the freedom you hold out to me. Help me take hold of it fully.

WISDOM

The Bible urges us to "Acquire wisdom! Acquire understanding!" (Proverbs 4:5). We are instructed to have two goals: Wisdom—knowing and doing right—and common sense. Wisdom is the ability to meet each situation with discernment and good judgment, whether in dealing with others, making choices, or dispensing justice. Wisdom involves using the knowledge we have to take the proper course of action—if we know and don't act, it is the same as not knowing at all. When we let Christ become the source of our wisdom, he will guide us in making wise decisions and acting on them.

When we really want to acquire wisdom, we must start by getting to know God better.

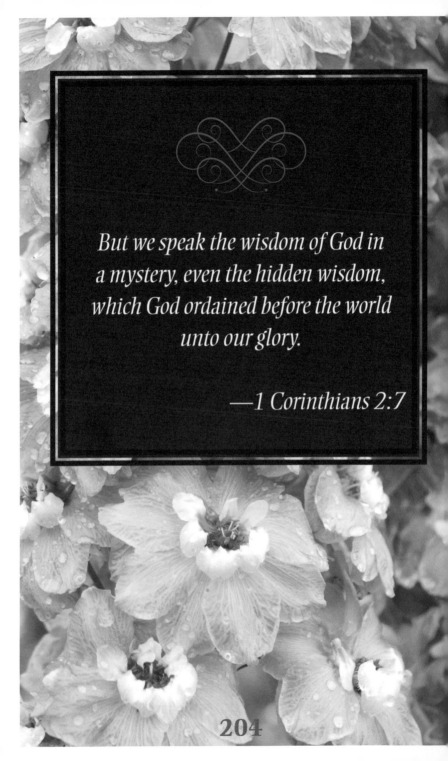

But we speak the wisdom of God in a mystery, even the hidden wisdom, which God ordained before the world unto our glory.

—1 Corinthians 2:7

God, I have such a limited perspective of the world. I have limited wisdom of how I should act in that world. Many times, when I've been unsure of what to do, you put an idea into my mind I never would have thought of, or gently nudge me to consider a solution I didn't even know existed. Your ways are such a mystery, yet I know that you know all and see all and therefore can help me live in a manner that goes far beyond the confines of my small view and often smaller expectations of what life can be like. Thank you, God, for always urging me to think higher, act higher, and live higher.

But the wisdom that is from above is first pure, then peaceable, gentle, and easy to be intreated, full of mercy and good fruits, without partiality, and without hypocrisy.

—James 3:17

When I read this verse, I realize how perfectly Jesus personified heavenly wisdom. It's a wonder to me that we are called to walk in his footsteps, but then I remember that it is only possible to do it through the Spirit that works in and through us. Thank you, Lord, for making the things of heaven available to those who seek them.

Let us hear the conclusion of the whole matter:
Fear God, and keep his commandments: for this
is the whole duty of man. For God shall bring
every work into judgment, with every secret thing,
whether it be good, or whether it be evil.

—Ecclesiastes 12:13–14

Many of us in this modern world prefer nutshell versions of things—CliffsNotes, abstracts, "just the facts, ma'am." Here in these two verses, wise King Solomon gives us his own nutshell version of what our existence is all about. After all his philosophizing and musing on life and its meaning, he boiled it down to two duties: (1) Fear God and (2) Obey his commands. Elsewhere in scripture we learn that all God's commands can be "nutshelled" into two simple commands: (1) Love God with all our being and (2) Love others by treating them as we would want to be treated. Lord, when I get confused about what living well is all about, help me remember to keep it simple, knowing my basic responsibilities are to revere you and love well.

But seek ye first the kingdom of God, and his righteousness; and all these things shall be added unto you.

—Matthew 6:33

Lord, you said to first seek your kingdom and all else will be given me. I tried for so long to seek those outer things first; those material things I thought would make me happy. And all it left me was feeling lost and alone and cold. But the kingdom you offer is one of love, mercy, and everlasting comfort. Your wisdom is far more precious than rubies and more priceless than gold. I understand that all good things can come to me only when I first immerse myself in your loving presence. That thought brings me a comfort nothing outside of me ever could. Thank you, Lord God.

> *Think not that I am come to destroy the law, or the prophets: I am not come to destroy, but to fulfill.*

—Matthew 5:17

Dear God, in my efforts to forge my own best path and be a role model, may I always respect those who raised children before me. May I not challenge convention simply for the sake of doing so, and may I always do so with respect and propriety. Lord, please keep me mindful of the example Jesus set: to respect the ways of his elders and ancestors. He did not come to destroy their ways but to uphold and better them.

Casting all your care upon him;
for he careth for you.

—*1 Peter 5:7*

I am the single mom of two teens. The last year has been challenging for me as a parent: my daughter has had a hard time adjusting to the rigors of high school academics, and my son has been testing boundaries when it comes to curfews and expectations at home. Some nights I am troubled by insomnia, and then the next day, I have a shorter fuse. Tempers flare. Dear Lord, please help me to remember that you are there for me. You are the answer to my anxiety. Help me to parent with wisdom and rely on you, even when I feel stressed and uncertain.

Who is wise, and he shall understand these things? prudent, and he shall know them? for the ways of the Lord are right, and the just shall walk in them: but the transgressors shall fall therein.

—Hosea 14:9

I am here right now, Father, because I do want to walk in your ways. I know the key is staying connected to you because the ways of the world are all around me, always imposing a different set of values and a different worldview. Give me a wise and discerning heart in all things today so I can stay on track.

Every word of God is pure: He is a shield unto them that put their trust in him.

—*Proverbs 30:5*

I have a friend who has read the Bible from cover to cover, and he described it as a profound experience. I have not read the Bible in this manner; I have favorite verses but, truth be told, the biblical prose can be intimidating. I do not always understand how the verses apply to my broken dishwasher or sick pet. And there are so many interpretations, sometimes conflicting, of what lies within the Bible's pages! God, grant me a clear, level head and an open heart so that I might understand the wise ways of your Word. May the rich stories, the adventures and drama and instruction that the Bible has to offer, be accessible to me. May I have the wisdom to apply its contents to my day-to-day life, and may I always be open to your teachings.

Call unto me, and I will answer thee, and show thee great and mighty things, which thou knowest not.

—Jeremiah 33:3

God, we know that pain has produced some wisdom in our lives, but it has also created cynicism and fear. People turn on us, reject us, hurt us, and none of us wants to play the fool more than once, so we're tempted to close off our hearts to people and to you. But relationships that bring meaning and joy require vulnerability. Help us trust you to be our truest friend and to lead us to the kind of community that will bring healing rather than destruction.

And God gave Solomon wisdom and understanding exceeding much, and largeness of heart, even as the sand that is on the sea shore.

—1 Kings 4:29

I don't have a lot of money, God, so when I think about giving to others, I often feel as though I have nothing of value to offer. Then I remember the times I sat with my grandparents before they passed away, listening to their stories and experiences, absorbing their wisdom, and cherishing their advice. I realized I have so much to offer to those around me. I have love and life experience and enough wisdom to help those who ask for it. I have a heart full of compassion and understanding. I have kindness. Thank you, God, for the gifts you instilled in me so I could pass them on to others...gifts no amount of money can buy.

Wisdom is the principal thing; therefore get wisdom: and with all thy getting get understanding.

—Proverbs 4:7

Not a day goes by when I don't do something without thinking, and regret it instantly. But I am trying, Lord. With all the distractions of life, I often act without first checking in with you and asking to discern your will and your wisdom. And, boy, do I pay the price for my ignorance and impatience when my problems get bigger, not smaller. But I am learning, Lord, and with each passing day I am stopping more often ask for your wisdom for whatever situation or challenge I may be facing. I've found that wisdom trumps quick knee-jerk reactions every time. Thank you, Lord, for helping me to understand it's okay to slow down and do the right thing and have no regrets about it later.

Let your speech be always with grace, seasoned with salt, that ye may know how ye ought to answer every man.

—Colossians 4:6

This world is full of people who have to be right, even if it means losing friendships or family connections. The need to be right causes so much suffering. Instead, seek the need to be wise. Seek the ability to use your God-given wisdom to be of help to others, and not a burden. No one is right all the time, and it takes wisdom to realize that and to learn to be compassionate to others, and to yourself.

Through wisdom is an house builded; and by understanding it is established: And by knowledge shall the chambers be filled with all precious and pleasant riches.

—*Proverbs 24:3–4*

Thank you for your wise ways, Lord. Following them fills my life with true blessings—the riches of love and relationship, joy and provision, peace and protection. I remember reading in your Word that whenever I ask for your wisdom from a faith-filled heart, you will give it, no holds barred. So I'll ask once again today for your insight and understanding as I build, using your blueprints.

Having knowledge is not the same as having wisdom. The true test of wisdom is knowing how and when to act, according to God's will.

If any of you lack wisdom, let him ask of God, that giveth to all men liberally, and upbraideth not; and it shall be given him.

—James 1:5

Well, Lord, since you're offering, I'm not going to be shy about asking. I need wisdom. I need it today as I'm dealing with people and situations and wondering what the best approach or decision might be. Thank you for being generous with your gifts rather than giving them to only a select few. In fact, you make receiving them as simple as just asking. You never cease to amaze me with your generosity, Lord. I'm deeply grateful.

The fear of the Lord is the beginning of knowledge: but fools despise wisdom and instruction.

—Proverbs 1:7

God, my children are entering their teenage years, a time when they might think they know best and are immune to tutelage. How many times of late have they responded to my suggestions with impatience or even scorn? Help me to guide them with patience—to remind them, in love, of the importance of remaining open to instruction. May they keep your essence a grounding influence as they learn and grow, and may I remember that, old as I am, I, too, must always remain open to what you and the world have to teach me. We are never "done," are we? Lord, help me to keep my love of God at the center of my journey of learning and teach my children to do the same.

He is like a man which built an house, and digged deep, and laid the foundation on a rock: and when the flood arose, the stream beat vehemently upon that house, and could not shake it: for it was founded upon a rock.

—*Luke 6:48*

Dear Lord, help me to build on a firm foundation by relying on your wisdom, diligently seeking your direction in all I do, learning to walk in your paths of kindness, peace, and justice to my fellowman.
In Jesus' name, Amen.

And they that be wise shall shine as the brightness of the firmament; and they that turn many to righteousness as the stars for ever and ever.

—Daniel 12:3

Let me do what lies clearly at hand, this very minute. Grant me the insight to see that too much planning for the future removes me from the present moment. And this is the only existence, the only calling I have been given—right now to do what is necessary. Nothing more, nothing less. Thus may I use this next moment wisely.

My brethren, count it all joy when ye fall into divers temptations; Knowing this, that the trying of your faith worketh patience.

—James 1:2–3

God, I give thanks for the wisdom you share with me when I am trying to understand my own actions or someone else's. You know what is best, and you have my highest good in mind. I will turn to you for the advice and guidance I need. Thank you, God, for being a strong and loving presence in my life. Amen.

God may throw us a few curves in life—we may feel hassled, troubled, anxious, or uncomfortable, and not understand why our circumstances don't fit our desires. But if we trust in the wisdom of his plan, God will provide for all our needs.

COMFORT

And I heard a great voice out of heaven saying, Behold, the tabernacle of God is with men, and he will dwell with them, and they shall be his people, and God himself shall be with them, and be their God.

—Revelation 21:3

Lord, on days when everything seems to go wrong, help me to remember that you are always nearby to offer comfort. It is easy to get overwhelmed and feel lost and alone in this world, but deep down I know that is never the case. You are always at the ready to help—I just need to remember to take a moment to stop, breathe, and pray.

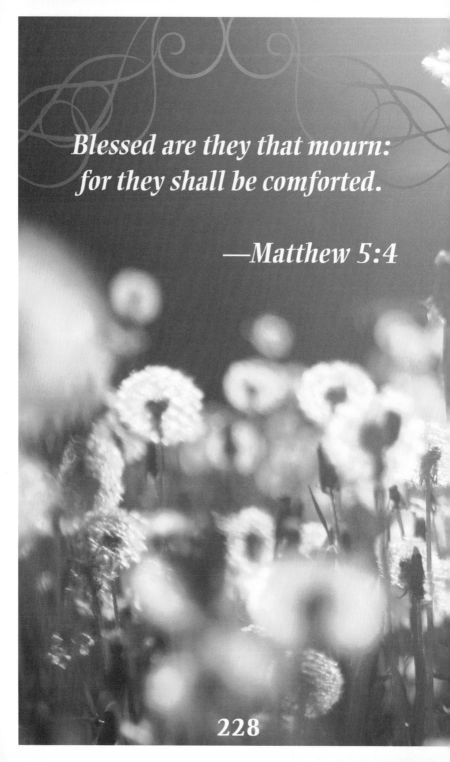

*Blessed are they that mourn:
for they shall be comforted.*

—Matthew 5:4

O Lord of comfort, only you know how deeply I am grieving. There are days when I don't know if I can get my breath, let alone face my responsibilities with a clear mind and a willing spirit. Come into my pain, Lord. Begin your miraculous healing from the inside out, because without you, I honestly don't think I'll survive this. Send your comfort, Lord, and caress me with your compassion. Amen.

Thy righteousness also, O God, is very high, who hast done great things: O God, who is like unto thee! Thou, which hast shewed me great and sore troubles, shalt quicken me again, and shalt bring me up again from the depths of the earth. Thou shalt increase my greatness, and comfort me on every side.

—Psalm 71:19–21

Thank you, Holy God, for your comfort in my time of need. Even when I am empty and near hopelessness, I know that you are there, eternal and gracious, giving me the will and strength to try again. Your love is a solace and a refuge, and I return to you over and over, seeking the renewing power of your Holy Spirit. Your grace refreshes and restores me, and I kneel at your feet in thanksgiving. Amen.

Comfort ye, comfort ye my people, saith your God.

—*Isaiah 40:1*

Lord, today I ask you to bless and comfort all who daily see pain and desperation as part of their jobs. Bless the social workers, Lord, and comfort them with the knowledge that what they do truly matters. Bless the doctors and nurses working with the seriously ill, and comfort them with your insight. Bless and comfort the caretakers toiling through the night, Lord, and send your strength to restore them. All these people are serving you as they serve others. Please give them your special blessing. Amen.

My soul, wait thou only upon God; for my expectation is from him. He only is my rock and my salvation: he is my defence; I shall not be moved. In God is my salvation and my glory: the rock of my strength, and my refuge, is in God.

—Psalm 62:5–7

Lord, when all else fails I know that I can count on you to be my fortress and my foundation. I give thanks each day for the steadfast comfort you provide, and I pray that you will give this same comfort to those who suffer in fear and silence today. Give to them the same freedom from worry as you did me, by showing them the same mercy and love you show me each day. Be their fortress just as you are mine so that they, too, may understand they never walk alone. Amen.

Blessed be God, even the Father of our Lord Jesus Christ, the Father of mercies, and the God of all comfort; Who comforteth us in all our tribulation, that we may be able to comfort them which are in any trouble, by the comfort wherewith we ourselves are comforted of God.

—*2 Corinthians 1:3–4*

God of comfort, help me lift my eyes and look beyond myself. What people around me are in need of your consolation? Have you given me this difficult experience to equip me to help them? Are there other ailing people who will listen to me because I know what they're going through? Are there people visiting me who are troubled by worries and fears? Are there doctors and nurses who are overworked and desperately needing a moment of joy or a word of love? Show me these needs and how I can meet them.

Let, I pray thee, thy
merciful kindness be for my
comfort, according to thy word
unto thy servant.

—Psalm 119:76

Lord, today I ask you to comfort the elderly among us. No matter how old we are, we notice our bodies aging. How difficult it must be to be near the end of life and struggling to hold on to mobility, vision, hearing, and wellness of being. Give us compassion for those older than we are, Lord, and thank you for your promise that you will be with us to the very end of our days.

But I would strengthen you with my mouth, and the moving of my lips should asswage your grief.

—Job 16:5

One of my oldest friends, Beth, recently and un-expectedly lost her husband. Dan was killed in a freak car accident, and Beth and her children have been blindsided by the loss. I have spent a lot of time with the family since the accident, and see how even the most well-meaning peo-ple have sometimes said hurtful things to Beth in their efforts to show concern. I want to avoid causing my friend any more pain, and so for the most part have tried to provide solace with my quiet presence. But I know that the right words can assuage grief. Dear Lord, grant me the wisdom to comfort my friends in their time of need. Help me to know what to say.

There shall not any man be able to stand before thee all the days of thy life: as I was with Moses, so I will be with thee: I will not fail thee, nor forsake thee.

—Joshua 1:5

Thank you, God, for never forsaking me, whether times are good or bad. In my life I have encountered all manner of people: lifelong friends, false friends, family who comforted me in my cradle and then stood beside me as I grew. But life brings change again and again. Friends move; death might take our loved ones; fair-weather relationships fade in the face of adversity or simply with time; children grow and, with the wings we gave them, leave our homes to make their own rich lives. These changes can be difficult—sad, disappointing, or even scary. As I grow older, I sometimes fear change and the loss it can bring. Help me to remember that you are always there for me, a rock, a friend, and a comfort all the days of my life.

Now therefore fear ye not:
I will nourish you, and your little ones.
And he comforted them, and
spake kindly unto them.

—*Genesis 50:21*

Money is a big issue for most people, and I am no exception. Either we don't have enough, or we worry about losing what we have. We are afraid of being left homeless and destitute. But God promises he will comfort and nourish us, with material things and things no amount of money can buy. God tells us not to be afraid. Dear God, I pray to worry less, and have more faith in your promise of prosperity. Even when my wallet looks empty, I know that blessings are happening in the unseen and will soon be made manifest. You never fail to sustain and support me, God of comfort. I pray for your care and comfort in good financial times and in bad.

Lord, I was just with my friend. You know the incredible hurt she is feeling right now. Please give me your wisdom and insight so that I can figure out how to lighten her burden—even if just a little. Show me, Lord, what I can say or do to help comfort her during this hard time. And during this struggle, may we grow closer in our friendship as we each also grow closer to you.

God promises us his comfort, but he also uses us as his agents to comfort others. In fact, the difficulties we've gone through often give us the ability to reassure others who are now going through the same experiences. How will God use you to extend comfort to someone else?

God does not comfort us to make us comfortable, but to make us comforters.

—John Henry Jowett

Dear God, comfort those whose eyes are filled with tears and those whose backs are near breaking with the weight of a heavy burden. Heal those whose hearts hold a wound and whose faith has been dealt a blow. Bless all who mourn and who despair. Help those who can't imagine how they'll make it through another day. For your goodness and mercy are enough for all the troubles in the world. Amen.

God, let me be a comfort to someone who needs me today. As you have always comforted me in rough times, let me do the same for someone who is sad, ill, or suffering and needs to know they are cared for. Guide me toward those I can be of loving service to, and let no opportunity pass me to do something good in the world today. If someone is in need, send him my way. If someone is depressed, have her call me. Let me be a comfort to those who feel they cannot go on alone. I am at your service today, God. Make use of me. Amen.

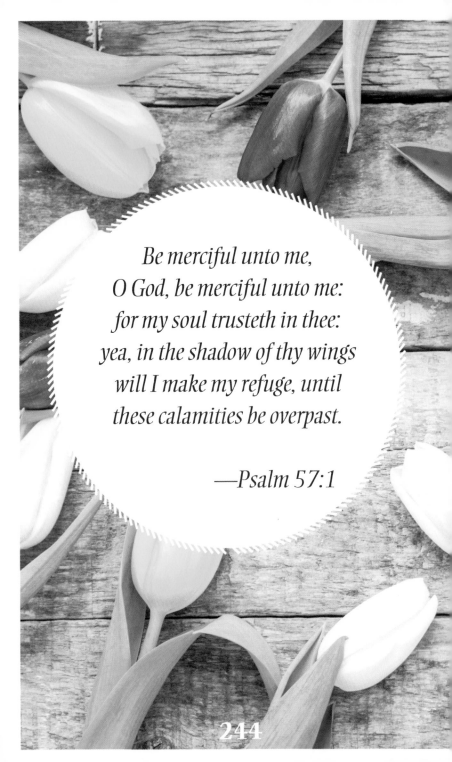

Be merciful unto me,
O God, be merciful unto me:
for my soul trusteth in thee:
yea, in the shadow of thy wings
will I make my refuge, until
these calamities be overpast.

—Psalm 57:1

God of all comfort, have mercy on me. I got angry today with my husband and accused him of not helping me enough. I scolded my child for talking too much. I shouted at the dog for barking too loud. And I almost hung up on my neighbor for taking up too much of my time with her problems. I need your comforting strength, dear God, wrapped around me like a soothing blanket, so that I can ask my family for forgiveness. Bless me with more patience, too, so that we don't have to go through all this again tomorrow. Thank you, God.

Let me find favour in thy sight, my lord; for that thou hast comforted me.

—Ruth 2:13

Holy One, I have striven to do what is right in your eyes. I have followed your word and obeyed your laws to the best of my ability. I now ask that you will be with me and comfort me. My needs are great and my power is small, but in you all things are possible. Please remove my burdens from me, for they are too heavy to carry without your help. Soothe me, love me, and care for me. I ask as your child, Amen.

But the Comforter, which is the Holy Ghost, whom the Father will send in my name, he shall teach you all things, and bring all things to your remembrance, whatsoever I have said unto you.

—John 14:26

Lord, I pray that my words and actions may be a comfort to those in need. Let me see the world around me through your eyes, so that I might notice the small wounds and sorrows that each of us carries within us, hidden from view and known only to you. I ask that you use my hands to do your work here on Earth, to heal the hurting, to feed the hungry, to befriend the lonely. May I be an instrument of your endless love, that I might share your spirit generously and abundantly with everyone I encounter. Amen.

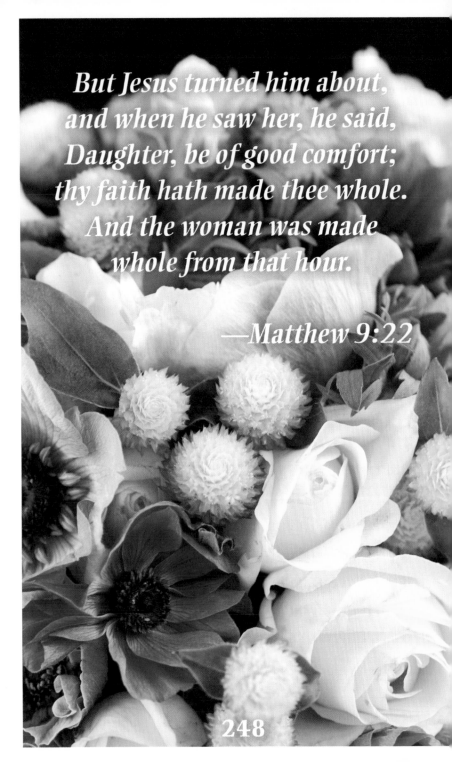

*But Jesus turned him about,
and when he saw her, he said,
Daughter, be of good comfort;
thy faith hath made thee whole.
And the woman was made
whole from that hour.*

—Matthew 9:22

Father in heaven, when all else fails, I turn to you for the comfort only you can provide. I have done all I can do, and now I rest in the belief that you are taking from me my burdens and doing for me what I cannot. In you alone do I find that comforting assurance that everything is being taken care of and that all will work out as it should. My surrender to your comfort is not out of weakness but out of my faith in your eternal love and concern for me. For that I am grateful.

SERVING OTHERS

For though I be free from all men, yet have I made myself servant unto all, that I might gain the more.

—*1 Corinthians 9:19*

Lord, my God, your son took on the role of a servant to all people. As a mother, I find myself walking in his footsteps. Service to my family has become life's greatest pleasure. I give myself willingly, not because someone demands that I serve but because I want to. As I cook and provide meals, wash clothes, and maintain my home as a place of comfort for my family, my heart sings with the joy of fulfillment. When I consider that no job was too lowly for Jesus, even scrubbing the floor brings me satisfaction. I thank and praise you, dear Father, for turning an independent person like me into a willing servant in your kingdom.

Blessed are the poor in spirit: for theirs is the kingdom of heaven.

—Matthew 5:3

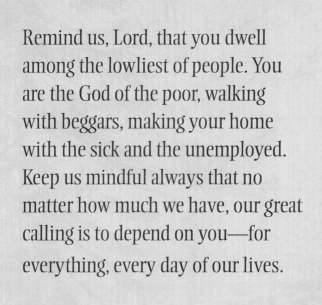

Remind us, Lord, that you dwell among the lowliest of people. You are the God of the poor, walking with beggars, making your home with the sick and the unemployed. Keep us mindful always that no matter how much we have, our great calling is to depend on you—for everything, every day of our lives.

Lord, thou hast heard the desire of the humble: thou wilt prepare their heart, thou wilt cause thine ear to hear: To judge the fatherless and the oppressed, that the man of the earth may no more oppress.

—Psalm 10:17–18

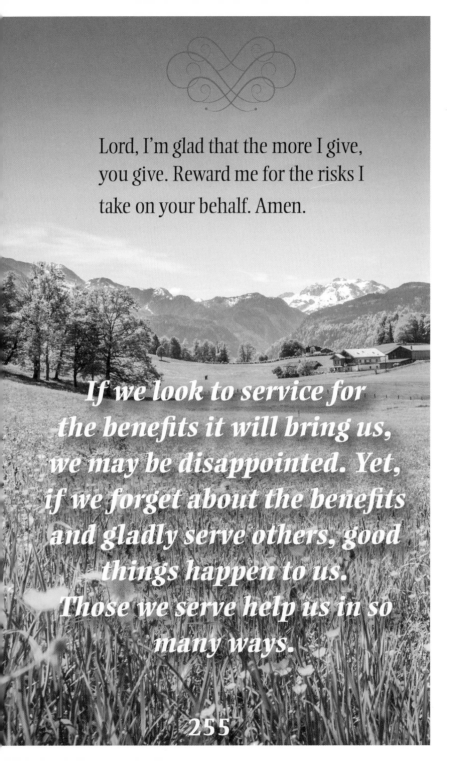

Lord, I'm glad that the more I give, you give. Reward me for the risks I take on your behalf. Amen.

If we look to service for the benefits it will bring us, we may be disappointed. Yet, if we forget about the benefits and gladly serve others, good things happen to us. Those we serve help us in so many ways.

For the oppression of the poor, for the sighing of the needy, now will I arise, saith the Lord; I will set him in safety from him that puffeth at him.

—*Psalm 12:5*

God, I look around my community today and I feel helpless. The homeless, the hurting, the needs each one represents are more than I can handle. But you can do it. You can meet each need. Teach me. Strengthen me and use me to serve as I reach out to my neighbor and meet just one need at a time!

"The Lord bless him!" Naomi said to her daughter-in-law. "He has not stopped showing his kindness to the living and the dead." She added, "That man is our close relative; he is one of our guardian-redeemers."

—Ruth 2:20

We are all connected, Lord, and may I impress upon my children the importance of this fact. It is one thing to talk about our connection to all living things but it is quite another to live it. Help me to demonstrate—not only in my words but also my actions—the fundamental role loving-kindness should play in our lives. Whether it is aid to an injured animal, support and a listening ear to one who grieves, or respectful words spoken about someone who is deceased, may I put good into the world without expectation of recognition or reward. May I do good simply for the sake of doing good, and may I never stop showing kindness to those in need.

Serve the Lord with gladness: come before his presence with singing.

—Psalm 100:2

To serve means to assist or be of use. Serving is one of the reasons we are on this earth and the reason Jesus himself said he came to the earth. When we serve, we reach out to meet the needs of others; service is an outward sign that we belong to God and desire to do his will. True service is not about grudgingly doing for others because of obligation, but an act that flows willingly, as a channel for God's love. True servants give not just with their hands, but with their hearts.

Then the disciples, every man according to his ability, determined to send relief unto the brethren which dwelt in Judaea.

—*Acts 11:29*

Father, it's easy to say, "Let me know if there's anything I can do." But how much better to peer closer, assess the situation to find what needs doing... then simply do it. Help me look into a friend's needs instead of waiting to be asked. Help me replace the words I utter so glibly with actions that might matter even more. Amen.

She stretcheth out her hand to the poor; yea, she reacheth forth her hands to the needy.

—Proverbs 31:20

Give me eyes, O God, to take a second look at those who think, act, and look different from me. Help me take seriously your image of them. Equip me with acceptance and courage as I hold out a welcoming hand, knowing that you are where strangers' hands meet.

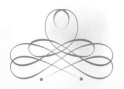

And I will pray the Father, and he shall give you another Comforter, that he may abide with you for ever.

—John 14:16

Dear heavenly Father, today, if I see or hear of someone who is struggling in some way, please help me take a moment to remember what it was like when I was struggling and you helped me through the aid of a friend or stranger. Let that memory mobilize me to offer help and be your true servant. This I pray. Amen.

Thou hast heard my voice: hide not thine ear at my breathing, at my cry.

—*Lamentations 3:56*

Today, Lord, you may call upon me to listen to someone and hear that person's heart. It may be someone who needs to feel significant enough to be heard, or perhaps someone who is lonely and longs to be connected to another person, or maybe someone who is hurting and needs a sympathetic ear. Whatever the case, Lord, please open my ears so I may listen to someone today.

Lord, help me to depend on you to be my source of goodness. I don't always feel like being patient, kind, loving, or joyful, but you are all of these things by your very nature. So right now I place my strengths and weaknesses into your hands, asking you to infuse them with yourself and to make them instruments of good that will serve others for your sake.

I am shocked by the treatment of the poor and needy in this country. Even people who claim to love God shun the poor and treat them as if they are less than human. It breaks my heart because God taught us to love everyone, including those less fortunate, and to reach out a helping hand to those in need. These are his ways, and so few live by them. God, I pray I never give in to greed and intolerance. I pray I always have an open and loving heart towards those who are struggling, no matter the reason for their struggle. That is not my reason to judge. All you ask of me, God, is that I love others as you love me. May I always be generous and giving to all of your beloved children.

Dear heavenly Father, I truly want to do good toward others. I don't want to just talk about being good, but I desire to be more compassionate. God, I need for you to teach me to be far more sensitive to the needs and sorrows of the people you have placed in my life and to be kind and encouraging toward them. I need for you to teach me how to truly love. I pray for this with all my heart. Amen.

Open thy mouth, judge righteously, and plead the cause of the poor and needy.

—Proverbs 31:9

When Ruth's friend Nora encouraged her to join in a neighborhood effort to go door to door and collect canned goods for the homeless, Ruth was at first hesitant; her natural shyness seemed to preclude such activity. But after praying and reflecting on her fears, she decided to move outside her comfort zone and help out. The experience was uplifting: it felt good to be acting—and speaking—on behalf of those in need. Lord, please embolden me to speak out for those less fortunate than myself.

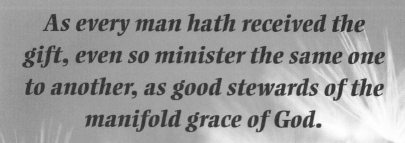

As every man hath received the gift, even so minister the same one to another, as good stewards of the manifold grace of God.

—1 Peter 4:10

Today I received a letter from a woman I am sponsoring in Rwanda through a Christian charity. It filled me with such joy and renewed my spirit. In the eight months I have been sponsoring her, I haven't bothered to write her a single letter. Receiving this letter prompted me to take the time to finally write to her. When I stopped to think about her situation, I also thought of my own life circumstances. Lord, I am a much-blessed woman and it is my duty as a Christian to pass on the gifts I have generously been given. Remind me that giving is about more than a monthly charge on my credit card. Let this connection with a woman less fortunate than me serve as a reminder of how much I gain by giving to others.

Serving others is the foundation of true gratitude.

Give, and it shall be given unto you;
good measure, pressed down, and shaken
together, and running over, shall men give
into your bosom. For with the same
measure that ye mete withal it shall be
measured to you again.

—Luke 6:38

We all have something to offer: time, money, expertise. God exhorts us to give generously; in his infinite wisdom, he understands that when we give, we're not just helping others (worthy in and of itself). But we also help ourselves. Studies have shown that generosity helps to manage personal stress, and have linked unselfishness and giving with a general sense of life satisfaction and a lower risk of early death. When we reach outside ourselves, we connect with others; God wants that connection, that sense of purpose and happiness, for each of us. Dear Lord, help us to connect with our best selves; help us to be generous givers.

And the King shall answer and say unto them, Verily I say unto you, Inasmuch as ye have done it unto one of the least of these my brethren, ye have done it unto me.

—Matthew 25:40

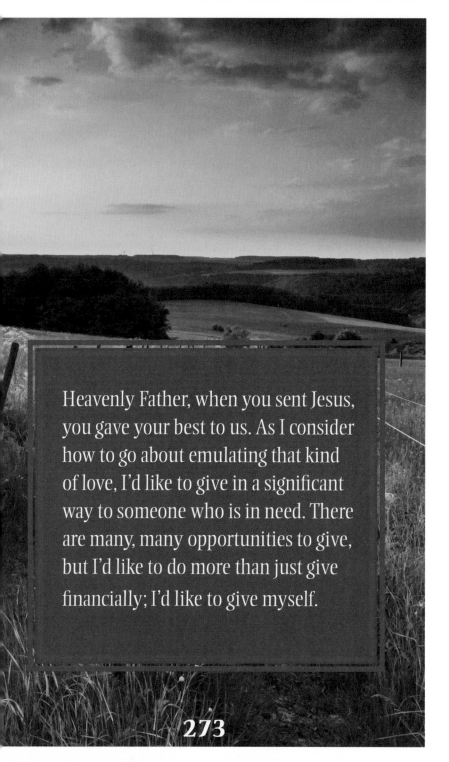

Heavenly Father, when you sent Jesus, you gave your best to us. As I consider how to go about emulating that kind of love, I'd like to give in a significant way to someone who is in need. There are many, many opportunities to give, but I'd like to do more than just give financially; I'd like to give myself.

FAITH

And the Lord, he it is that doth go before thee; he will be with thee, he will not fail thee, neither forsake thee: fear not, neither be dismayed.

—Deuteronomy 31:8

Lord, give me the faith to take the next step, even when I don't know what lies ahead. Give me the assurance that even if I stumble and fall, you'll pick me up and put me back on the path. And give me the confidence that, even if I lose faith, you will never lose me.

The Lord will perfect that which concerneth me: thy mercy, O Lord, endureth for ever: forsake not the works of thine own hands.

—Psalm 138:8

Lord, if there is one thing I can use more of, it is faith. Good, strong, solid faith. Faith in the harmony and order of a world I can't comprehend. Faith in the goodness of a society I often feel distrust for. Faith that my family will be protected and loved, even when I am not there to protect and love them. Most of all, dear Lord, I need faith in myself and in my abilities to grow as a woman, a wife, and a mother. So give me not diamonds or fancy cars. Those I can do without. Give me faith. Good, strong, solid faith. Amen.

Fight the good fight of faith, lay hold on eternal life, whereunto thou art also called, and hast professed a good profession before many witnesses.

—1 Timothy 6:12

I wonder who can really have faith in good anymore with so much bad in the world. Seeing the death and destruction makes me question my own faith, God. I am sorry to admit that. This is when I most need to turn to you in prayer, God, and to ask not just for help coping, but help in recovering my faith. I know your ways are mysterious, and I cannot understand them, but please help me turn back to faith when fear threatens to overtake me. There is so much love and good out there, God. Keep my eyes on the sun, and when darkness comes, keep my heart focused on your light to guide me through the night.

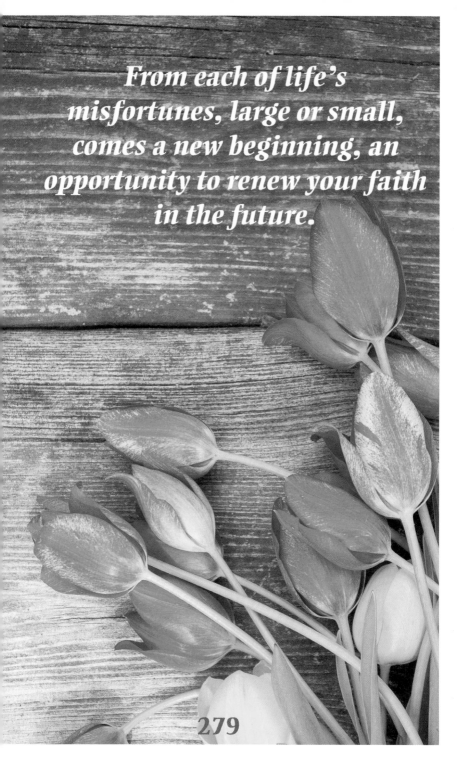

From each of life's misfortunes, large or small, comes a new beginning, an opportunity to renew your faith in the future.

And I say unto you, Ask, and it shall be given you; seek, and ye shall find; knock, and it shall be opened unto you. For every one that asketh receiveth; and he that seeketh findeth; and to him that knocketh it shall be opened.

—*Luke 11:9–10*

Lord, I know you will show your goodness and faithfulness to me if I just diligently seek you. The problem isn't your willingness to give, but my tendency to try to do everything by myself rather than leaning on and trusting in you. This silly inclination brings me needless stress and wastes precious time. Today I endeavor to lay my needs and troubles at your feet the minute I begin to feel the least bit overwhelmed.

Faith is the substance of things hoped for, the evidence of things not seen.

—Hebrews 11:1

Heavenly Father, what do I have to fear when you are the one caring for me? And yet, I do fear. Irrationally I fear, despite your faithfulness, despite your assurances, and despite your promises. Why do I still fear? I don't always understand my trembling heart and the shadows of things far smaller than you before which it cowers. Please liberate me from these lapses of trust. Free me to stand fearlessly, supported by faith and hope, in the center of your great love for me.

Thou art my hiding place; thou shalt preserve me from trouble; thou shalt compass me about with songs of deliverance.

—Psalm 32:7

O Lord, how often I turn to you when I don't know where else to turn! If only I would always turn to you first. My faith in you is a constant in my life, and yet too often I let other influences distract me and lead me away from a total reliance on you. I know in my heart that it is in you, and you only, that I am protected and safe. Shelter me, Lord. You are the only place I want to run in times of trouble. My faith rests in you.

Trust in the Lord with all thine heart; and lean not unto thine own understanding.

—Proverbs 3:5

Sometimes I work so hard to control everything that I need to be reminded to take faith and "let go." Last night my head was in a whirl: I lay in bed and stared into the darkness, worrying about bills, my workload, if my husband and I would have time to care for the yard before the frost. My mind churned as I envisioned schemes, schedules, emails I might write, ways to exert control. It was only when I "let go" and decided to give my concerns over to you that I earned some measure of peace, and was able to sleep. Lord, thank you for your support and guidance as I navigate my busy days. May I have the faith to trust you over my own understanding.

*There is therefore now no
condemnation to them which are in
Christ Jesus, who walk not after the flesh,
but after the Spirit. For the law of the
Spirit of life in Christ Jesus hath made
me free from the law of sin and death.*

—Romans 8:1–2

Lord, how I long to stand strong in the faith!
I read of the martyrs of old and question
my own loyalty and courage. Would I, if my
life hung in the balance, say, "Yes, I believe
in God"? I pray I would, Lord. Continue to
prepare me for any opportunity to stand firm
for what I know to be true. To live without
conviction is hardly to live at all.

But without faith it is impossible to please him: for he that cometh to God must believe that he is, and that he is a rewarder of them that diligently seek him.

—Hebrews 11:6

Lord, I must deal with people every day who don't have any faith in you, in life, or in themselves. All they do is whine and complain, and it saps my energy. They only believe in what they can see, and what they see is pain and fear and worry. I know telling them to have faith in you won't help. So I ask that you use me as an example of how joyous and peaceful life can be when you do the driving. Let the rewards and blessings you've bestowed on me serve as a reminder of what having simple faith can do for someone who is lost, alone, and afraid.

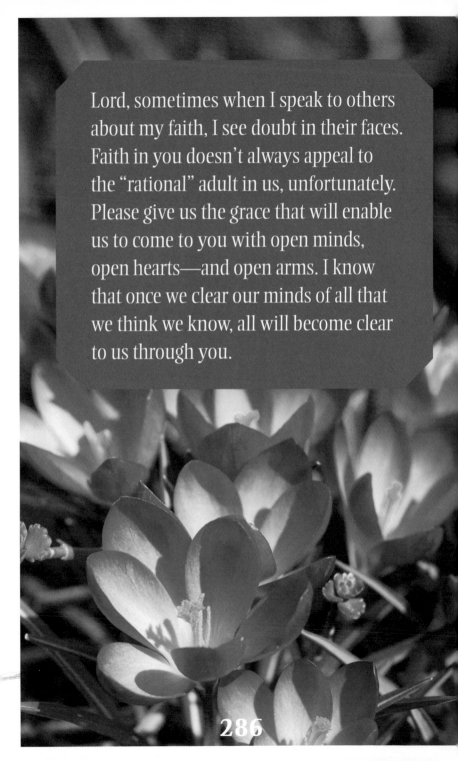

Lord, sometimes when I speak to others about my faith, I see doubt in their faces. Faith in you doesn't always appeal to the "rational" adult in us, unfortunately. Please give us the grace that will enable us to come to you with open minds, open hearts—and open arms. I know that once we clear our minds of all that we think we know, all will become clear to us through you.

Wherefore, if God so clothe the grass of the field, which to day is, and to morrow is cast into the oven, shall not he much more clothe you, O ye of little faith?

—Matthew 6:30

I am so tired of worrying, God, about how to pay the bills, how to keep the kids safe, how to keep my friendships and marriage healthy. I feel so defeated at times, when it appears that the dark is overwhelming the light, and evil is so prevalent over good. Help me, God. Help me to refocus and relax in my faith and to remember that things are not always as they seem. Help me to remember all the ways you have come through for me. Help me to stand taller in faith instead of shrinking in fear before the ways of the world. Help restore my faith, God.

But let him ask in faith, nothing wavering.
For he that wavereth is like a wave of the
sea driven with the wind and tossed.

—*James 1:6*

God, it is hard to have faith all the time these days, especially when I lost my job. Money is tight and I don't know how I am going to support my family. I know that your ways are much higher than mine, and your plan for me is one I cannot imagine, but I need help during these dark times to keep my solid foundation of faith intact. My children depend on me and look up to me as a model of a strong and faithful woman. Show me how, dear God, I can be the best role model for my kids. Help me solidify my own faith, so that I can be the best mom and person I can be.

But sanctify the Lord God in your hearts: and be ready always to give an answer to every man that asketh you a reason of the hope that is in you with meekness and fear.

—1 Peter 3:15

Serena and her husband Jim moved to their new home during winter, and she'd looked forward to the neighborhood's annual summer block party. She figured she'd meet new people; what she didn't anticipate was that her faith might be challenged. "So you're one of those religious types?" a woman laughed, upon learning that Serena and Jim attended a church nearby. Though uncomfortable, Serena dug deep: "Yes," she responded with polite firmness. "We've found happiness in our new church home." Dear Lord, sometimes I am asked to justify my faith; sometimes I am even mocked for it. Please strengthen my heart and give me the right words and spirit to articulate my belief.

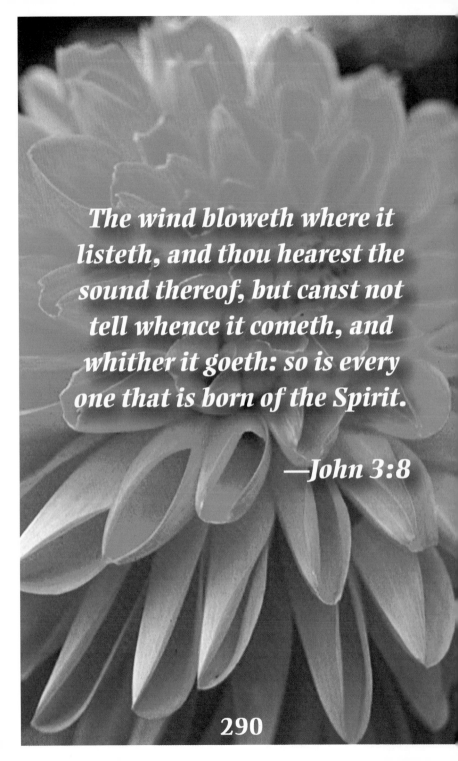

The wind bloweth where it listeth, and thou hearest the sound thereof, but canst not tell whence it cometh, and whither it goeth: so is every one that is born of the Spirit.

—John 3:8

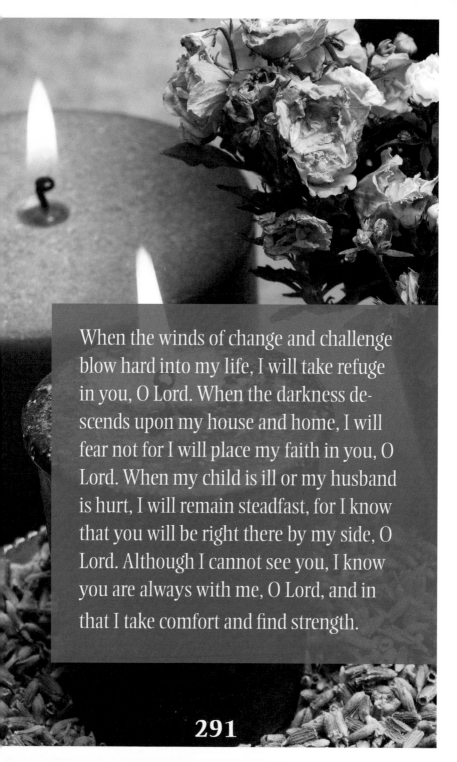

When the winds of change and challenge blow hard into my life, I will take refuge in you, O Lord. When the darkness descends upon my house and home, I will fear not for I will place my faith in you, O Lord. When my child is ill or my husband is hurt, I will remain steadfast, for I know that you will be right there by my side, O Lord. Although I cannot see you, I know you are always with me, O Lord, and in that I take comfort and find strength.

I remember someone saying that what doesn't make us bitter will make us better. Lord, I've never seen the good in becoming bitter about life. Your grace is always big enough for each of us, whether our trials are few or many. I want to become better, though, when I come through a painful struggle, a difficulty, or a loss. Help me remember that the work of making me better is your work. My work is to remain faithful to you—trusting in you. From within that place of trust, you will fashion a better kind of faith, hope, and love within me.

Know therefore that the Lord thy God, he is God, the faithful God, which keepeth covenant and mercy with them that love him and keep his commandments to a thousand generations.

—Deuteronomy 7:9

We are creatures of habit, with default settings that bring us back to anxiety and fear every time we are presented with a new obstacle or challenge. Isn't that the truth? I know I do that. I forget you have never abandoned me, God, and sink into depression or worry at the drop of a hat. I know you are faithful to me, and unceasingly so. Why can I not be more unceasingly faithful to you? I aspire to know and experience more of your grace, and to be an example of a strong faithful person to my family. Forgive me for the times I forget you never turn away from me, God, even though I may turn away from you.

Help us, O Lord our God; for we rest on thee, and in thy name we go against this multitude. O Lord, thou art our God; let no man prevail against thee.

—*2 Chronicles 14:11*

Sometimes the "multitude" we face is a multitude of pain, a multitude of trouble, a multitude of opposition from others, or a multitude of sadness. When it feels as though there is a multitude of something that is too big for us, threatening to distress us, what can we do? There is only one who is bigger and more powerful than anyone or anything else in life. Let us remember today that our God is for us, and his power is greater than that of any multitude. My Lord and my God, in you I stand today against the multitude that would seek to discourage my faith. In every circumstance that threatens to overwhelm me, please grant me your peace as you exercise your power to protect me.

*Then shall thy light break
forth as the morning, and thine health
shall spring forth speedily: and thy
righteousness shall go before thee; the
glory of the Lord shall be thy reward.*

—*Isaiah 58:8*

I have faith in you, Lord Jesus, for you have
never let me down. My faith makes me
strong and fills me with the courage and
fortitude I need to get through life's more
pressing problems. Your faith in me is like
a beacon that I move toward, helping my
eyes focus on the prize of your love and on
your assistance in all that I do. Knowing
that I am not alone helps me be a pillar of
strength for others as well, as they discover
their own lost faith in you. I have faith in
you, Lord. You always come through for
me. Thank you.

Lord, I am weary and cannot find my way. The nights seem endless and thick with a fog that engulfs my spirit, but I have faith in you, my Lord and my light. Faith that you will help me take another step when I feel I can no longer walk on my own. Faith that you will be the beacon of hope that guides my way through the darkness. Faith that this, too, shall pass and that I will know joy again. Amen.

There are many events in our lives over which we have no control. However, we do have a choice either to endure trying times and press on or to give up. The secret of survival, whether or not we question God's presence or his ability to help us, is remembering that our hope is in the fairness, goodness, and justice of God. When we put our trust in the character of a God who cannot fail us, we will remain faithful. Our trust and faithfulness produce the endurance that sees us through the "tough stuff" we all face in this life.

Faith is a living, daring confidence in God's grace. It is so sure and certain that a man could stake his life on it a thousand times.

—Martin Luther

Lord, we are a people in search of a shortcut. Give us the five-minute dinner preparation and the instant credit. But we know, because you are so clear about this in your Word, that a mature faith can't be achieved overnight. Give us patience to endure, Lord. We are determined to become the complete individuals you intended us to be.

We never outgrow our need for faith. No one is too strong, too mature, or too experienced to benefit from its grace.

Therefore I say unto you, Take no thought for your life, what ye shall eat, or what ye shall drink; nor yet for your body, what ye shall put on. Is not the life more than meat, and the body than raiment?

—Matthew 6:25

Loving God, I confess that I worry too much. I worry about the welfare of my children. I worry about my husband's job. I worry about our budget, which buckles under the weight of our growing family. I even worry about worrying! Forgive my doubts, my lack of faith and trust in you, O Lord. Teach me to express my family's needs to you daily in prayer and to trust in your ability to supply them. In my heart I know you will never let us down. With you in charge of our lives, we will want for nothing, for you take care of all your creations.

HARD TIMES

But if any provide not for his own,
and specially for those of his own house,
he hath denied the faith, and is worse
than an infidel.

—1 Timothy 5:8

As a woman, I have to work twice as hard to balance the needs of my family and my job. My income helps the household, so I cannot stop working. But being a great mom and wife is the most important job there is. I go to bed most nights exhausted and worn down trying to juggle both. God, I pray for the extra energy and strength needed to get done what needs to be done at work, with plenty left over for the ones who love and depend on me at home. I pray for balance in my life and the wisdom to know what to do when home and work are both tugging at me for my attention.

Blessed be God, which hath not turned away my prayer, nor his mercy from me.

—*Psalm 66:20*

I've set a single place at the table, O God, and am dining for the first time without my companion, my lost friend. What can we say to bless this lonely meal? What words can we use to grace this half-portion of life? Be with me as I swallow around lonely tears. Bless my remembering; inspire me to care for myself in honor of all the love that went before. May I live with this loss, always leaning on you for strength, even when I can finally stand alone.

Strength and honour are her clothing; and she shall rejoice in time to come. She openeth her mouth with wisdom; and in her tongue is the law of kindness.

—Proverbs 31:25–26

Some chapters in life are more difficult than others. My mother—who has been a confidante, a support, and a role model my entire life—was recently diagnosed with dementia. Dementia is a long goodbye, and even as I grieve this loss and help her navigate a very scary new chapter, I am determined to remain present for my husband and our two children. Some days, I struggle against feeling ground down and bitter. Many days, I am angry that this disease is robbing me of my wise mother, and my children of the grandmother they have known. God, I am afraid. Please help me to remain steadfast and honorable in my actions, no matter what turns life takes in the days ahead.

And let us not be weary in well doing: for in due season we shall reap, if we faint not.

—Galatians 6:9

Nancy's brother Ed has suffered from depression for years. He's on medication now, which helps. And Nancy tries to uplift him (and sometimes succeeds) with daily texts, movie nights together, and the occasional dinner out. "Ed's depression has been a learning experience for me," Nancy shares. "I can be there for him, I can't stop trying, but I cannot expect that every one of my efforts will make a difference. I have to be at peace with that." Lord, I am discouraged because my efforts to help others seem to mean little. Help me to not lose heart. Help me to keep trying.

I recently graduated from college, and while I look for a job in my field of study, which is geology, I've been working a series of lower-paying jobs to pay the bills. I have managed to create a life I'm proud of. I pride myself on being independent and not living beyond my means. But my student loan debt is substantial, and there are not too many miles left on the old car I've been driving since high school. My current jobs do not offer health insurance. Some days I feel discouraged that I have not yet found the work for which my education has prepared me. Some nights I can't sleep for worrying about finances, or what expenses lie around the corner. God, help me to remember that you are there: to support me, and imbue me with strength and wisdom. Help me to remember that you will provide.

Ye shall seek me, and find me, when ye shall search for me with all your heart.

—Jeremiah 29:13

God, today I am mired in the challenges that life can bring. My mother is losing her battle with cancer. I try to be strong and supportive—for Mom as well as for my children—but inside I feel such fear. What will I do without her? How will I help my daughters navigate this loss? I know that you are there, but I feel depleted and alone, Lord. I do not always have the strength to seek you out. Please embolden my heart to always search after your own.

Above all, taking the shield of faith,
wherewith ye shall be able to quench
all the fiery darts of the wicked.

—Ephesians 6:16

Today I face a frightening health issue, God, and I am more afraid than I would like to admit. Nobody wants illness. Nobody wants to go under the knife or be told they may not live to see their children grow up. But I have you, God, and with your presence today, I know I can get through any challenge. I know I can stand up to the fear and the worry and vanquish it with love and faith. I know you don't give me more than I can handle, God, and that you'll be there to handle it with me nonetheless. Thank you, God, for being my shield and my rock and my faithful warrior.

But exhort one another daily, while it is called To day; lest any of you be hardened through the deceitfulness of sin.

—*Hebrews 3:13*

Robin loves her brother Jim; she also knows he struggles with a gambling addiction. The siblings were driving together to a wedding, and their travels took them past a casino. Jim wanted to stop. Robin didn't want conflict, but she stood firm. "It was hard for me to confront him, but we actually had a good talk," Robin says now. "And we didn't go to the casino. That day, Jim needed me to help him do the right thing." Dear God, please be with me. When I see someone tempted or vulnerable, help me to reach out and offer encouragement.

For with God nothing shall be impossible.

—Luke 1:37

I am enduring a dark period, God. Alzheimer's disease ravages my beloved father, and I must assist him and my mother while I try to raise my own three children with strength, patience, and joy. Some nights I lie awake, filled with fear that my little family will not survive this next chapter—one of many "Sandwich Generation" families with children and parents to care for. Dear God, help me remain faithful to the promise that with you, nothing is impossible, even if I can't see through it for myself.

O thou afflicted,
tossed with tempest, and not
comforted, behold, I will lay
thy stones with fair colours,
and lay thy foundations
with sapphires.

—Isaiah 54:11

O Lord God, this horrible disaster has really been a blow to my family and me. It was so unexpected. One day, everything is fine, and the next day, everything is gone. Our extended family, friends, and church all want to help us, and we are truly grateful for their generous compassion, but still we feel utterly defeated. A lifetime of hard work is wiped out, and now we have to start over. Please help us, Lord, to be thankful that we have our lives and each other, and most importantly, that we have you to take care of us. Help us, we pray in Jesus' precious name. Amen.

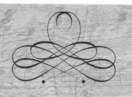

Behold, I will bring it health and cure, and I will cure them, and will reveal unto them the abundance of peace and truth.

—*Jeremiah 33:6*

Mental illness can be so devastating, Lord. Few understand the heartaches involved in diseases that carry no apparent physical scars. Be with those friends, neighbors, and family members who deal daily with difficult situations of which we are often unaware. Touch them with your special love, and let them know that they can lean on you, Lord. Ease their burdens, quell their sadness, and calm their desperation. Bring comfort and healing to these households.

God hears my cries for help, and
He answers every prayer.
I only need be patient—
He supplies the "how" and "where."

Sometimes it may be immediate
In a tangible way I'll know;
While other times I wait assured
That he is strengthening my soul.

His grace is all-sufficient
To meet my heart-cries need.
As I lean upon his promises,
Walking in faith, he'll lead.

Brethren, I count not myself to have apprehended: but this one thing I do, forgetting those things which are behind, and reaching forth unto those things which are before, I press toward the mark for the prize of the high calling of God in Christ Jesus.

—Philippians 3:13–14

After graduating high school, Anna took a year off to work and earn money for university. "Sometimes it's a little lonely," Anna admits. "Many of my friends have already gone on to college." On low days, Anna feels left behind, but then she reminds herself that this is her path, it's a good one, and that God supports her, always. "God has my back," Anna says simply. "That comforts me." God, you are my best coach! I don't need to reach higher alone; thank you for being there to inspire me.

SPAIN